Amber's Reflections

A Candid Personal Conversation About Cancer, Hair Loss and Empowerment

With an introduction by Peggy Miller

© 2015 by Peggy Miller. All rights reserved.

No part of this book may be reproduced, stored in retrieval systems, or transmitted in any form or by any means, electronic, mechanical, photocopying, recording, or otherwise, without the prior written permission of the publisher, except in the case of brief quotations in a review or article.

All inquiries should be addressed to:

Images Unlimited Publishing
P.O. Box 305
Maryville, MO 64468
660-582-4279
info@imagesunlimitedpub.com
http://www.imagesunlimitedpublishing.com

Front cover and interior layout design: Teresa Carter
Cover and interior photos: Birmingham family

ISBN 978-0-930643-32-4

Library of Congress Cataloging-in-Publication Data

Birmingham, Amber Nicole, 1984-2010.
    Amber's reflections : a candid personal conversation about cancer, hair loss and empowerment / with an introduction by Peggy Miller. -- First edition.
        84 pages cm
   ISBN 978-0-930643-32-4 (paperback)
 1. Birmingham, Amber Nicole, 1984-2010. 2. Birmingham, Amber Nicole, 1984-2010--Philosophy. 3. Osteosarcoma--Patients--Biography. 4. Young women--United States--Biography. 5. Terminally ill--Psychology. 6. Loss (Psychology) 7. Self-actualization (Psychology) I. Title.
   RC280.B6B57 2015
   616.99'4710092--dc23
    [B]
                                          2015012290

First Edition

Printing 10 9 8 7 6 5 4 3 2 1

Printed in the United States of America

Dedication

To Amber's mother, father, grandparents, aunts, uncles, cousins and friends, including her boyfriend, George, and her beloved cat, Ricardo.

We were all touched in a personal and unique way by Amber Nicole Birmingham. Yet, we all agree that by knowing her we have a deeper understanding of the purpose and meaning of life.

Table of Contents

Introduction 7

Amber Nicole Birmingham 11

Loss 13

The Beginning—2008 15

It's Back—2009 29

Expectations—2010 52

It is Done—2010 77

A Poem by Amber 79

Acknowledgements and Updates 81

About the Author 82

Introduction

This book is a vehicle for sharing the life of Amber Nicole Birmingham (1984–2010) and her reflections with others. I have prepared this collection of Amber's writings because I was overwhelmed by her insight and growing self-actualization during her battle with osteosarcoma, a type of cancer that starts in the bones.

Along her journey I encouraged Amber to write and share her thoughts with others. Bob and Barb Newhart and Carmen Davis also encouraged Amber to collect her writings and share them with others.

Amber touched so many in so many different ways; one has to believe she was a young adult with the wisdom far beyond her youthful age.

I read Amber's thoughts in her email messages many times before I was ready to assemble this book. During this time I was reminded of a concept from a philosophy class years ago that helped me understand Amber and her efforts to help others understand. The study from the class inferred that the meaning of one's life and existence was to find one's own special gifts. Once those gifts were found, one's purpose was to give those gifts away. I believe Amber fulfilled this philosophical belief.

A deeper understanding of Amber's thoughts and gifts began during my initial meeting with local publisher, Lee Jackson. When I shared my story about Amber, Lee informed me she had just ordered some amber jewelry for her daughter-in-law. She continued to tell me that many people believe the amber stone has healing power for those who wear it. Babies often wear amber beads around their necks during painful teething episodes and some persons use the stone to neutralize their arthritic pain. This semi-precious stone is sometimes referred to as a "window of the past."

Lee went on to share a reference book on gemstones, **Modern Jeweler's Consumer Guide to Colored Gemstones**. Here the characteristics described for the amber stone include the ability to:

- mix humor and adaptability
- remain calm in stressful situations
- facilitate family bonding
- promote strength and a greater awareness of self
- enhance artistic abilities.

These characteristics provide an uncanny description of Amber. The history and folklore associated with the stone became a perfect way for me to describe her.

The author of the reference book went on to state that the companion stone for amber is the crystal. I immediately thought about the reflective nature of the crystal and thought of Amber's ability to reflect and derive deeper meaning to everyday experiences.

This relationship between the amber stone and the crystal made sense to me as I began to compare characteristics of the stones to my understanding of Amber. It became a perfect way to explain and present the thoughts and writings of my niece, Amber Birmingham.

Amber's Reflections emerged as the perfect title for this collection of writings. I predict that the reader will soon realize and appreciate the wisdom and insight reflected in Amber's writings.

Additional comments and personal messages from family and friends have been included throughout Amber's writings. Only the responses of individuals who provided a signed consent to include their thoughts and personal identification have been included. Due to space, not every response provided was added. I have chosen to keep the writings of Amber and those of family and friends in their original format. There are also blank spaces included for the reader to write personal comments and thoughts.

In addition to reflecting back on the life of Amber, I believe this would be an important resource for others in many fields. Those working through social services, medical services, hospice programs, and family life education will find this information meaningful.

Peggy Miller
"Aunt Peggy"

Amber Nicole Birmingham

Amber Nicole Birmingham was born in Des Moines, Iowa on October 25, 1984. Amber was the only child of her parents, Terry and Joelyn Birmingham. Amber and her parents enjoyed a typical family life and in my opinion, had a family bond that strengthened each day they shared. I observed this bond grow stronger and sustain this family during the biggest struggle of their lives–osteosarcoma.

I watched loving care and support flow from Amber's parents, her grandparents, Max and Janet Miller, Ben and Eden Thornely, Don and Bonnie Birmingham as well as aunts, uncles, cousins and friends. Her beloved cat, Ricardo, and her boyfriend, George, provided Amber with unconditional love and support.

Amber graduated from Indianola High School in 2003. She and her parents enjoyed the typical school-age and teen years. As Amber grew older more and more people began to appreciate her quick but honest sense of humor. I recognized that there were some characteristics of Amber's thinking that appeared to me to be beyond her young age. Friends described Amber as having an ever forgiving spirit. These traits became so obvious to me and others as we participated and communicated with Amber on her care pages established by the University of Iowa Hospital system in Iowa City, Iowa.

Additional financial and emotional support came from Amber's extended family at the Legion Post 232 from Polk City, Iowa. The post members initiated the annual *Ride it Out for Amber* motorcycle rides to increase awareness and provide resources for research in the area of osteosarcoma. The members of Post 232 were and remain a large extended family support group for Amber's parents.

I recall one story when one of the members was seriously injured on his bike. Amber and her parents visited him in the hospital and found him down emotionally as well as physically. Amber was able to motivate him to face the challenge and work hard in taking an active positive approach toward getting better. And he did. He provided a very touching and heartfelt testimonial at Amber's funeral.

Amber's family, along with the Legion Post, continues Amber's fight for a cure for this cancer. These efforts have become a family mission and an important way to carry on Amber's legacy.

Osteosarcoma is a malignant bone tumor that can develop in teenagers and/or young adults. It apparently takes advantage of growth spurts and periods of rapid bone growth to attack. However, this affliction is not uncommon in late adulthood and in aging populations. An exact cause of osteosarcoma is not known but one's predisposition may be found in family genetics.

In Amber's case, the osteosarcoma originated around her knee. Pain and discomfort from an apparent knee injury in September, 2007 and a second injury to the same knee in December, 2007, ended with a diagnosis of osteosarcoma in January, 2008. And so Amber's journey began.

Dr. Mohammed Milheim, MBBS from the University of Iowa Hospital and Clinic became the primary doctor and coordinator of the army of specialists dedicated to help Amber and her family through this illness. Better known as Dr. Mo, he was always there for Amber and communicated often with her family about treatment as well as her over-all well-being. Dr. Mo is a clinical Associate Professor of Internal Medicine specializing in oncology and blood and marrow transportation.

Dr. Mo provided "state of the art" medical advice and guidance. He supported a multidisciplinary approach to his treatment of sarcoma with the central goal always being to improve his patient's treatment and quality of life. More importantly, Dr. Mo provided love and support to Amber and her family during her battles and remains in contact with the family to this day. He can even be observed participating in some of the *Ride it Out for Amber* events. Special support with long lasting effects was also provided to Amber by a special nurse named Wendee Baranek.

Loss

Loss occurs for everyone. Loss has no boundaries of race, gender, ethnicity, capability, or age. Loss is experienced when one's abilities change or when a position of employment or supervision is removed. We see loss of strength, power, and even our physical stature. Subtle but still, loss occurs when we begin to forget things or can't recall a name or the face of a special friend. But the loss that brings about the most change and impact on our lives is the loss of a friend or a beloved family member.

One never gets "used" to this type of loss; but through our faith, our grief eventually supports the ability to endure. Somehow we incorporate that person totally into our thoughts and memories. They become such an important part of us. We are able to smile more often when we talk about our memories–but we never get over missing them.

My family lost a special person long before her time. However, I am convinced that although very young, Amber Birmingham was a very seasoned and wise soul. Her spirit still shares many of the lessons she was able to provide for us.

It is almost impossible for me to understand how a person so young was capable of facing her own tremendous losses with such dignity. She lost her freedom to flow in and out of friendships and relationships with her friends. She lost her capability of moving smoothly with her body and the joy of always feeling good. She lost her control over her hair style and important things that young women like to do. She lost her dreams of finding that special person and of a making a home for a family.

Amber lost so much but gained an insight far ahead of her age on earth and formed a faith much stronger than most of us possess. We know we will NEVER lose Amber and increasingly appreciate and understand what she gave to us in such a short time.

I have paraphrased the following statement as it represents the way I felt as I read and re-read Amber's thoughts.

> If you listen very closely,
> you can hear the flutter of angel wings,
> and know that Amber is still near.

Reflection 1
The Beginning—February 2, 2008

Hello everyone. It's Amber. My parents and I made this page so family and a few close friends could feel more involved in the whole process of helping me go through this cancer. For those of you who don't already know, the official name of this is "Osteosarcoma". It's growing from my right knee and today it rises about 2 inches from my leg. That's much smaller than it started out so it's good.

This whole thing started around September when I was moving some furniture. We thought I'd sprained my knee. A repeat injury in December is what sent me to an MRI and we found the tumor. Since then I've been through MANY more scans, lots of pokes, and uncountable doctor visits, but I've been blessed to have you all around me and praying for me constantly.

I had my first chemotherapy treatment on January 26th. It's been a real experiment this first time because we're learning what makes me sick and what doesn't. After that first treatment I was REALLY sick to my stomach for about a week. Today is the first day I have felt well enough to get up, use the computer, eat and drink frequently, etc.. . . I feel really good today.

This page is here so everyone can feel involved and say whatever they would like to say, so please feel free to leave any questions, comments, or concerns on here. My family will check it in the weeks after my chemo when I am not able to. We set it up so the notices go to their email too. My hope is that this will help everyone ease some of their concerns a little more.

Once again, I appreciate all the love and support that is pouring in right now. I never find myself alone for long, or without someone to talk to when I can talk. My parents have been great when I've been a vegetable, and the gifts, cards, donations, and flowers that have shown up here have been so touching to all of us. So thank you once more for that.

Response Messages

By Ed Birmingham

Hey Ber, I am really glad you are feeling better. The girls ask about you every day, this will help me keep them informed. We are all here for you and your family and we want to help, don't hesitate to ask. Love Uncle Ed and the girls

By Tina Brown

AmberCrombie this is a fabulous idea. We (the entire clan), want to stay involved and help you get better! Let us know when we can help in any way–Terry–that means you have to let us!

By Al Appenzeller

Hi Amber,
(Al, Mel, TJ and Hana) are all praying and pulling for you! We are also so very proud of you! Remember God is always with you and so are we! Don't forget about that hot air balloon ride I promised you as soon as you feel up to it and the weather is nice! The Appenzeller family

By Sandy Baker

Have a Great Valentine's Day Sister! I hope you have an awesome Valentine's Day and get something really awesome. Oh wait, you already did–that beautiful necklace from your momma and daddy. It was so nice to have you come to dinner with us, we'll do it again really soon. Try to relax and enjoy your Valentine's Day. Just know that we will be praying this next Chemo goes smoother than the 1st one. We love you girl!

By Eden Thornley

Amber, I think this is great. You are being a real trooper, you know how some of us are about our hair, and it would take your Dad to help. We would like to come over to IC to see you on Saturday if it is OK. Is there anything we could bring? What kind of books do you like? Any special author? Love ya lots Grandma and Grandpa Thornley

By Marsha Snethen

We love you Dipper head! You are in our thoughts and prayers every day and you are a very special person. I know my life is better because of you. I am always here for you. Love always

By Becky Carter

XOXOXO From the Carters–We love you Amber and wanted to let you know if you need any more KFC mashed potatoes you just give me a call and I will put them in my contact list on speed dial for you. I love you and hope this weekend goes smoothly for you. Let us know if there is anything you need and we will send it up with Grandma. And remember you are Beautiful!!!!!

By Angie Pauscher

Thinking of you Amber. We have all been thinking of you. We are very proud of you for being so strong and brave! We are praying for you every day and at my prayer group. You have a big circle of family who are all thinking of you even though we haven't all been together for a while. Just know you have a lot of love around you. Keep your head up and put all you trust in Jesus. Love Mike, Angie, Jordan, Natalie and Sydney Pauscher

By Ed Birmingham

Hey Ber, sounds like things are a little better this time that is SO good. The girls ask about you every day. This web site is great. Oh and by the way...everyone likes my new haircut. (shaved his head like several others) I may keep it this way for a while. If it wasn't so *****cold. We all love ya Amber and mom and dad–you guys rock!

By Julie Kaestner

Hey Amber! I'm just thinking about you and wanted to let you know that I feel really positive about tomorrow. I know that it may not seem like much, but I've heard how your positive thinking has been helping you to cope so I thought that maybe it would work for me too. You've been a very courageous young lady the past few months and I have learned a lot more about you by watching you struggle and triumph! You've been awesome! Tomorrow you WILL triumph! Keep up the positive thinking for tomorrow and I'll see you there! We love you! Aunt Julie and the crew

By Sonja Templeton

Hey Sweetie. So glad to hear that you are keeping your spirits and attitude up. You are a strong young woman!!! Tiff and I keep each other updated so I'll let her know you've been feeling a bit better minus the lack of appetite. Throughout my day I think of you and your family often . . . keep hanging in there!

By Callie Freeman

I was looking for a picture of beans–in memory of singing that song outside grandma Helen's on the porch swing. Thanks for teaching us that song Amber; it's one of those talents you try to keep a secret. Hope you're feeling better–I'd like to see some of those paintings you were going to do. Love you Callie.

Reflection 2
Going Back to the Hospital—February 11, 2008

Hello everyone. It's Amber again. This will probably be my last update before going back to the hospital on Friday. I will have another CT scan of my chest that day and then start the 2nd round of chemotherapy. This week I finally started losing my hair. It was pretty devastating the day I went in and started brushing it and it started coming out in massive chunks. There were a few tears, but nothing Dad couldn't make me laugh off. It has continued to fall out every day since then, and I'm starting to show bald spots. Mom's cousin, Marsha came over Sunday night and cut it short to hopefully slow the process down. I'll probably shave it when I get out of the hospital because I imagine it will be pretty spotty looking by then.

Another first for me was a full body massage from my mom's friend. She did it for free for me, and it was really really wonderful. It helped me relax and not think about pain for a while. She is doing it again on Thursday so I'm nice and relaxed before my chemotherapy treatment.

Other than the CT scan and the chemo treatment, that's all the updates I have for now. Physically I'm feeling good today. I went to my house and did some packing for a few hours. I'm going to try to go out to dinner with a friend tomorrow night. Plus Mom is going to go in to Michaels and pick up some paints and canvas for me so I can get back into painting these days that I feel good. I'm really excited about painting again. It's something I've had to put aside for so long, but it really makes me feel good. So the next update should be from Mom. Enjoy the pictures of all the head shavers!

By Monty Freeman

Hello Amber, Jo and Terry–Thanks for including us in this website information. We got on as soon as we got your email. We have been thinking about you from the beginning Amber, and now we can send a message to you as well. You are so brave and have been such a trooper going through all of this. We have rejoiced every time we've heard that you made a step forward. You are in our prayers, always. Keep your positive thoughts and attitude. Thanks again for providing us with this website. Love Lori, Monty, Callie and Kelsey

By Al Appenzeller

Hi Amber, It was so nice to hear the good news and to know you get a small break from Chemo. Please just take some of this time to enjoy those things you really like to do. We pray for you regularly and praying for all of your doctors and wonderful health care providers too. Love Mel, T.J. and Hana

Reflection 3
Another Surgery—March 31, 2008

Hello again–it's Amber. I finally made it back to the computer! There's not much to report other than what Mom said in the last update. I still have quite a bit of pain in my leg, and I'm afraid they'll take me off the painkiller medicine before my pain is gone. That's my biggest fear at this point.

I posted a new picture on here as well. I think I took that last week on my cell phone. I haven't wanted anyone to take pictures of me since I lost my hair, but I decided it might be ok if I took the picture myself, just to see how it would look. It's still not Miss America, but it's a start. I can't wait to have hair again though!

I have pictures of some T-shirts Tyler and Kenzie had made, but at the present time, I'm not able to get them on here. There's a problem with the file size I guess. Once I get that figured out, you can all see the shirts though. They're really cool.

Also Mom ordered a bunch of yellow ribbons if anyone wants one. There are over 200 of them, so feel free to take as many as you'd like.

Response Message

By Julie Kaestner

Hey! Ooooh! A whole new knee! How exciting! Honestly though, we'll be praying for you. You've been a trooper and I'm sooooo happy for you that soon you will be good as new. We love you and will definitely be thinking of you. You've proven that you can do anything, so once again, keep smiling. Love Aunt Julie

Reflection 4
Making Progress—May 4, 2008

Hello everyone. It's Amber again. I finally feel good after Chemo #3! Yesterday and the day before were HORRIBLE. I couldn't get comfortable in ANY position. I felt nauseous too. My chemo doctor decided I needed to go get my finger pricked, which revealed that I needed platelets. I was supposed to go to Methodist Hospital for that, but they never called. Finally, yesterday afternoon, my mom contacted my chemo doctor again and asked when this was supposed to take place. He was pretty upset that Methodist hadn't called, so he sent me to the ER. I had to get re-tested, and finally received the platelets. Mom was pretty grouchy because they always screw up around there, but I was finally comfortable for some reason! So I curled up with a pillow and was singing her some Pink Floyd and questioning her about random 80's music lyrics. I was amused, but she may not have been. Someone may want to get her that WOW-80's CD. She was a little rusty. Lol

Aunt Becky came over last night and watched "Men in Black" with me too. Thanks Aunt Becky. Once I feel better from chemo, I hate sitting here alone all the time–even if I AM only watching a movie!

The latest development is now I've got Mom playing "Sorry" with me. We're trying to talk Dad into playing but so far no luck. We're now accepting additional people to beg Dad to play a board game with us. Lol

So after the whole platelet incident–I am back on the road to recovery. Next doctor visit is Tuesday–with the surgeon who removed my tumor. The goal is the bending of my knee soon. I think that's a big part of why I couldn't get comfortable for 2 days. There are only SO many positions you can get in without moving your right leg!

Response Messages

By Peggy Miller

Good Morning Amber. I am so excited to be able to keep in touch on the care page. I sent the sun because we finally have a sunny day to celebrate your good news. I talked with your grandpa yesterday on his birthday and he said you had just left the birthday party. Sorry I missed you. Hope the news continues to be so GREAT! Love Aunt Peggy

By Barb Freeman

I was so glad to hear that your surgery went well and it sounds like you are beating this thing. I also want to thank your mom for sending me the address for your Care page. You've had quite a fight so far and have fought hard. Keep up the good work and we are praying for you. I think things will just go up from now on. Please know that we think of you often. Love, Aunt Barb and Uncle Austin

Note from Amber

Thanks for the prayer shawls! I curled up with the one you made for mom and it's so soft–like curling up with a kitten or something! I appreciate the time and prayers that go into making those–and the happy tears of course! See you when Sam is better.

Note from Amber

Physical Therapy–that walk to the door was probably the hardest steps I'll ever take! I'm just glad I had some people there who supported me. The steps are a lot easier every day thank God! Sorry I had to cry in front of Sienna though…she was probably worried. Just tell her I'll be playing barbies and coloring in no time.

Reflection 5
Just a Little Something I Wrote—October 11, 2008

Hi everyone. I wrote this last week. It's actually a posting for my blog on cancer website, so it's more directed at the people on there who have cancer, but Mom thought I should share it with everyone else too. It's not a literary masterpiece–just what I was thinking about at the time. And before you read it remember–no tears. The worst is over now and I'm ok! I'm a phone call/email away, instead of a prayer away. Love Amber

The Loss of Something Beautiful
By Amber Birmingham, October 7, 2008

My hair has been rapidly growing back for almost 3 months now, and 99% of the time, I am excited about it. I take off my hat and Mom laughs and comments on how fast it's growing, everyone that has seen it is so happy for me. . . . But then there's that 1% of the time that I still find myself mourning my OLD hair–my REAL hair. This nearly BALD chick isn't me at all! Where is that girl with the long shampoo commercial hair? And when will she be back? Although I don't think about it frequently, I still feel horribly vain. And when other people want to hear my cancer story, I find that the chapter where I shaved my head is almost always left out, because I've only been able to tell the story without crying once, because it very literally broke my heart to shave off the hair I'd taken such meticulous care of for 23 years.

Since I'm in the privacy of my own living room and no one can see me cry, perhaps now would be a good time to share the head shaving chapter. (Hell I started crying halfway through the first paragraph of this post lol)

I had been warned that my hair would fall out when I was first diagnosed and the chemo regimen was started, so from the very first moment they started the chemo, I was watching for it. I would sometimes tug on my hair a little just to make sure it was still firmly stuck on my head. And for the entire first round of chemo, and the following 3 weeks, it was securely stuck. I was thrilled! I thought maybe I'd be one of the lucky ones and wouldn't suffer that particular side effect. After 3 weeks I had round 2 of chemo. After that I just didn't feel well at all, so I kept my hair in a ponytail all the time. One day while my parents were at work (I had to move back in with them temporarily during treatment) I took my pony tail out and there was an alarming amount of hair stuck in the rubber band. My heart told me it was starting to fall out, but my head insisted on denying it. I was only allowed the luxury of denial for about another week or so. My mom's cousin (a former beautician) volunteered to come over and cut my hair.

Everyone had told us that it would be easier to adjust to losing all my hair if I cut it first. It'd be more gradual. I remember pulling my hair over my shoulder and kissing it good-bye before she cut it. Nobody saw that because I felt so stupid kissing HAIR. She cut it to my chin, but in the process of brushing it out just so she could cut it; most of it came out anyway.

2 days passed with big chunks of hair falling out every time I'd take my pony tail down. The top of my head was completely bald. I didn't feel pretty anymore. My Dad kept volunteering to shave my head for me. And he'd say I should just get it over with and then I wouldn't have to worry about it coming out anymore. He made it sound so EASY–and he was so right. But getting there was so painful. Finally I got my parents to sit down with me and just talk about it. All 3 of us cried that night. After 2 hours of talking, I finally had enough resolve to walk out to the kitchen and let Dad shave what was left of my hair. I grabbed a towel and bawled into it almost hysterically for the first few minutes. My hands were shaking. I felt sick. And

as luck would have it, the razor got stuck. I guess that's what you get for using a beard trimmer to shave a head.

By the time he was half way done, an odd calm had come over me. And when he finished, I put on my hat, and refused to look in the mirror. A friend/boyfriend called a few minutes later, and we talked for a long time about other things. And while he was still on the phone, I finally went in the bathroom and glanced in the mirror. And it was . . . somewhat ok. I didn't think much at all when I took the first look, but I was grateful to have someone on the other end of that phone.

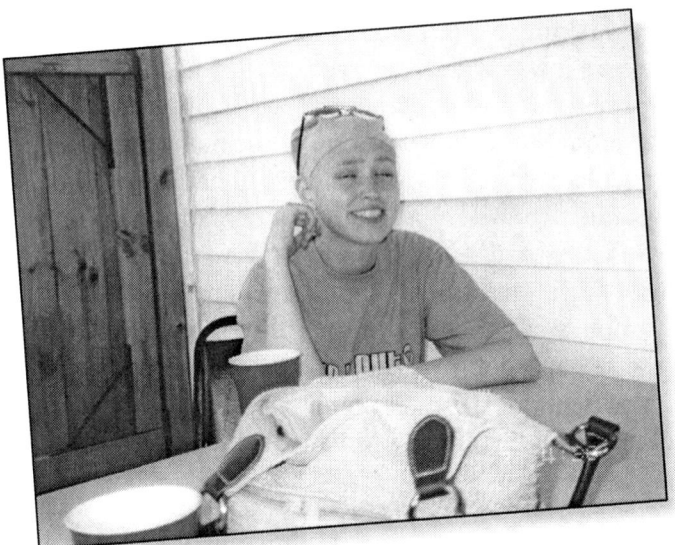

Amber in a sunny spot.

Shaving my head that night was the boldest, more empowering thing I ever did in my life–and probably the most empowering thing I ever WILL do. It allowed me to take control of the situation that was out of control for the first time in my life, and THAT was good. But even with that said, it is definitely not JUST hair.

So there's my story. I've shed enough tears writing it, that I might have enough water for the cat (KIDDING!). So what's everyone else's hair loss/head shaving story? I wonder if it's different for guys and girls. I certainly wasn't obsessed with any part of my appearance before, so that's why I find it so strange that I had so much trouble with losing my hair. Hope to hear

I'm not alone actually! PS—as for the current hair situation—I've got about a centimeter now. At that rate I'm going to look like Aerosmith in no time.

Response Message

By Barbie Freeman

Hi Amber (and Terry and Joelyn), I don't know if this makes any sense to you, but it occurred to me and so I thought I'd share. One of the things that I learned throughout the journey following my niece's murder in 2007 and up to the trial in 2009 for the perpetrator, is that there are times that words seem so pale and inadequate that one doesn't know what to say. Yet, most of us want to say something and we wish we could say just the thing that would make a difference–that might make your journey a little more tolerable. When that happens, sometimes people say nothing, fearing they'll say the wrong thing. Sometimes people say really dumb, unhelpful things in an attempt to offer something. What I found most helpful, was the people who simply told me "I don't know what to say, but I wish I did." Knowing that the sentiment was offered sincerely meant a lot. Of course people don't know what to say! Sometimes such unspeakable things happen in our lives that all anyone can do is tell us they care and that they will bear witness with us to the pain so that we don't have to bear it alone. So, I want you to know that I do bear witness to your suffering and continue to pray for your strength and healing on this journey of disbelief. Barbie Freeman

Reflection 6
Surviving—December 28, 2008

Last night was not a good night. I learned that my friend in Australia just passed away from osteosarcoma. He was diagnosed and treated at age 10, and it came back when he was about 16 and had already spread to his lungs and brain. He was 17 years old when he died. I can't help but think how this same thing could happen to me. The threat of the cancer returning is ALWAYS hanging over my head. I would almost venture to say I am obsessed with the thought. It haunts me when I'm awake AND asleep. I try to live every day to the fullest and not live in fear, but sometimes I fail miserably at it.

I am fairly certain God spared me for a reason, but have no idea what that reason IS yet. I find myself feeling like I'm wasting what little time I have left by NOT knowing what I'm supposed to be doing in my life. And how much time DO I have? I know that nobody is certain of when they will die, but I sure wish I could stop thinking about it. The way my friend died was the absolute definition of a "slow and painful death" that most people fear. They sent him home to die in July and his vision went, and then his hearing. He had panic attacks frequently because he knew it was coming. He lost the ability to walk. And then–at the very end, he got kidney stones. And they couldn't laser them because he didn't want to endure one last surgery. He KNEW it was over for him, so he just kept the kidney stones for another 2 weeks until he died. I'm just terrified to go that way. Since I MUST die someday, I wish it would be a fast death and I wish I could be an old woman when it happens. There's just so much I want to do here.

Well I hope I didn't just make everyone sad with this. I tend to get a little raw when I write (hence the reason MOM wrote most of the updates lol) It IS sad though. This is the harsh sad reality of cancer. It never REALLY goes away, even if you've been given a clean bill of health. Cancer is with me ALWAYS. You never forget where you've been, or your fear of going back.

The good news is that I sent my oncologist a panic-stricken email at about 2 in the morning, and he wrote back that I can keep getting scans for the rest of my life if I want, so we can stay on top of it so we'll know if it DOES come back, so hopefully it won't spread to my brain like it did with my friend. He told me not to worry. He assured me that we will be diligent in watching for any signs of my cancer returning.

I love Dr. Mo; all is right with the world after talking to him. My hope is that I can help everyone else understand OTHER people who have gone through cancer–not just me. Trust me—from my conversations with other people with cancer—they're ALL thinking this. We can all love and support one another better if we understand what they're going through.

Response Messages

By Barb Newhart

Hi Amber. I'm so sorry to hear about your friend. It only makes sense that you have those thoughts and fears. I have to say it's true that once I've heard the "all clear" about you and others, I have just gone on with my life, and not given another thought to the daily reprieve that you seek. You have a real gift of writing, that's for sure. I agree that it is very difficult to determine what the lesson is that God has for us. I just now that we can't plan the outcome, but simply pray each day to follow His will for us. I also know that can be a tough thing to do every day! Please continue to keep us updated.

By Barbie Freeman

Amber I'm so sorry to hear about your friend's death. You're awfully young to have endured so much and to have lost someone you cared about. I'm sorry for that too. You did a wonderful job sharing your fears and joys. I'm glad you have such a wide circle of support. I was sorry that the Miller Christmas got cancelled due to ice. It's understandable, but disappointing. It would've been nice to see you and everyone else that we haven't seen in so long. Take care.

By Marsha Snethen

Oh Amber, I hope and pray that you can get past this, but it is hard when you have friends that pass away. With experience–time will heal and as time passes you will always think about it, but it won't be as fearful. We will always pray that it will NEVER come back and you will be here to see me get old. We love you very much and if you ever need anything, please let me know. Keep your head up and everything will be fine. Love Ya–Marsha

By Peggy Miller

Amber, I read your post yesterday and have thought of you constantly ever since. I do know that some of your purpose is to give others the faith and courage to continue a battle when all looks so bleak. What a purpose you are serving. Not knowing our purpose exactly–is really part of the mystery of God's miracles. You are indeed a part of His miracle. Thank you for all you give to others and we all continue to send our prayers for your healing and peace. Love Aunt Peggy

By Mary Miller

So sorry to hear of this, our thoughts and prayers for you continue. Love Royden & Mary

By Sandy Baker

Okay sister, as I keep telling you, we are going to BELIEVE that this crap will be over sooner not later. You WILL be able to move on and do ALL the things you have wanted to do without having to look over your shoulder in fear of this stinking cancer. We BELIEVE that God has given this team of doctors the gift to heal, well; God has already done the healing.

Reflection 7
It's Back—July 24, 2009

So I'm back in the hospital getting chemo again. I'd finally worked myself back up into a positive mood. I'd gone to sleep last night, and then I was awakened by a nurse. We ended up getting a private room this time. Anyway, the nurse asked me if I'd be willing to switch rooms with a woman who was "actively dying." I said yes of course. Then I asked, "Does the woman KNOW she's dying?" and the nurse said, "Yes she does. I think her passing will be a relief to her family though."

And then I started bawling. Not because I was giving up the private room, but for some woman in another room, whom I'd never met and never WILL meet. Cancer got her too. Just like so many others. The nurse hugged me hard. She said, "But you're NOT dying, because you're here taking chemo and you're going to beat this!"

I said, "But there's just so much death around me lately! I can't take it all! And I just can't stand that cancer is taking one more away!" As is turned out, the woman's family decided not to move her in the middle of the night, and the nurse said a private room would probably open up during the day. I wouldn't have to move at all. So that was the end of THAT.

But . . . I cried for a long time still. And then I woke up today, and I cried some more. I think I really could've done without hearing about another person dying to this. I know it HAPPENS, But still . . . I still feel really weak emotionally after hearing that. Does anyone else struggle with this—not being ok with hearing when someone dies from cancer—but then thinking you're avoiding reality?

I don't know. I know reality is something we must all face, but I can't handle this particular reality right now. Death is DEFINITELY too close to home right now. And I feel weird for sobbing over a person I'll never know. It was one of those rare times when I cried without fully understanding why. Thanks for listening everyone.

Response Messages

By Barb Newhart

You are NOT weird. I don't think I can say it any more eloquently than the others already have. You are definitely a courageous woman, one who I admire greatly. You have immense strength in the face of this monster. And, I agree that there's nothing wrong with focusing on brighter things when what surrounds us is dark. I think of you and your folks daily, and you're all in my prayers. You're gonna lick this baby!

By Peggy Miller

Dear Amber, I have been thinking so much about your thought and your compassion for the woman you "did not" know. I think the more each of us grows and experiences life, the more we do know and understand the joy and the pain of others. I think your tears and the release they provided for you reflect your concern and identification with the woman you "did not" know. Amber, you DO know her more than most of us could ever possibly know her. God has given you the ability to be responsive. A virtue many never obtain. I think my closest experience to yours, is the loss of close friends, my age mates. This also has a way of bringing reality about life clearly to mind. It makes us cry. And that is alright.

These experiences, similar to yours in a small way, have a purpose. Embrace life and live each moment fully. God has great plans for you Amber, so build your positive energies toward your own recovery. You are indeed loved by so many, and our thoughts and prayers are there with you constantly. Love Aunt Peggy

By Barbie Freeman

Amber, I applaud your honesty and willingness to be so open and vulnerable about not wanting to deal with reality and then feeling guilty about it. For what it's worth, I think it makes sense that you would feel sad and overwhelmed. It makes sense, to me anyway, that you are feeling less resilient because you have been coping for some time now with difficult realities that require lots of energy. Setting boundaries between you and how much reality/grief/stress you come in contact with seems wise.

I already shared with you about my niece being murdered a few years ago. It was a huge trauma for me and my family. While that was all going on (being played out in the media and legal system), Brad was laid off from a job of 11 years. He found another within 7 months only to be laid off from that. He has now been out of work for over a year. I have found that the stressors on my plate are at times overwhelming and that compartmentalizing and setting boundaries about what I allow into my consciousness are not only normal, but very important. I don't watch the news or read the paper–too many people losing jobs and suffering in too many ways. Of course, I can't put my head in the sand completely, but I can take care of myself by choosing some of what goes on that plate.

I don't know if any of this resonates with you or not, and I'm certainly not comparing my challenges to yours, but I hope it offers some peace. Barbie Freeman

Reflection 8
Waiting—August 20, 2009

Hey everyone, It's Amber. A lot of people have been asking me to update my Facebook more, or give some sort of update here. But I got hit with something about a month ago, and I've been dealing with it on top of cancer (I'm sorry, but I don't want to say what it was). I haven't said much to anyone–just kind of drifted around the world with the conversation in my mind going on and not bothering to share any of that conversation with anyone. So to the worriers–I'm really sorry. To the people who haven't noticed–HEY! How ya doin?)

As for the conversation–I've been thinking negatively lately. I didn't want to splash negativity all over everyone else, so I kept it to myself. I've walked around talking to God in my head almost non-stop. I've been begging and pleading for a miracle. I was watching TV with grandma in Missouri, trying to find something she'd like (which is basically flipping through the channels looking for something I WON'T like! Lol joke) and I found this church service (on Saturday NIGHT? OK whatever I'll think about that later). The church service was about healing and they talked about God's spirit needing to come upon you. They said a lot of things that confused me. I was frustrated and felt like I'd been doing something wrong all this time. I went to bed and couldn't sleep hours later. I prayed and prayed because it's all I could do there in the darkness—pray for my broken body, broken heart, and broken spirit. THEN—for one quick second, I felt it. The spirit. And I (being a total IDIOT) prayed for healing, and these kids I know–they were on my mind and I just wanted them to be ok.

So for days I thought about that–silently of course. Please understand that I have to think something completely through before I can blog or talk about it. I realized I should've LISTENED instead of TALKED at that time, and I kicked myself for that.

Anyway, back in Iowa, I did a ton of fun stuff that Mom has probably told you all about, but the funk just wouldn't lift! When those 3 things are broken in combination, it's just hard to face …EVERYTHING–Ugh. I dug deep trying to keep faith, because I AM a fighter. I've SEEN a miraculous healing. Why on Earth am I so worried this time?

Anyway, I needed platelets yesterday. I got them at 8 a.m. and they gave me Benadryl. It was great. It knocked me out. I took a nap when I got home, and then went back out with Mom, but the Benadryl made me so out of it, that I FINALLY didn't care about anything for an ENTIRE DAY. I leaned my head against the window of the car and JUST enjoyed the trees flying by and the sky…I haven't felt like that for over 2 years now. Benadryl–the breakfast of champions???? Probably not. But it allowed my heart to stop racing, my mind to slow down, and my spirit to go run around with the fairies somewhere, or whatever spirits do in their down time (mine runs with fairies ok!) It doesn't like to go clubbing.

So the official update–I just woke up. Physically I feel great. Inside I'm fighting very VERY hard to keep faith and keep some sort of positive-ness coming out of me. I'm trying to make myself "be ok" with whatever the scan results are on Thursday. This is like trying to swallow a live deer while it's still kicking. Try it sometime. No fun. Leaves you with a sore throat. But I won't let you all down.

Oh–and God came back a few nights ago. That time I listened. I got no guidance–but about 2 seconds of peace. Don't give up on me just yet. I'm not.

Reflection 9
Mayo Clinic—September 13, 2009

As most of you know, we saw the new oncologist at Mayo Clinic in Minnesota–Dr. Okono. We saw him on Thursday. We were told to stick around another day and see the surgeon on Friday. Don't even ask me what his name was. I'm lucky I remembered the Japanese oncologist's name. Lol

So I text messaged and Facebooked a bunch of people because I finally had GOOD news. I was ecstatic! Finally, I had an update that I knew would generate "smileys", and "that's great!" And "congratulations", instead of–well, they're not nice words to use in front of ladies, but yes there were some profane responses to prior bad news, none of which offended me. I was angry too at those times. Trust me–the "F" bomb was exploding with great fanfare in my mind.

Thursday night I had a headache from all the pent-up tension I'd had before visiting the oncologist, so I was able to fall asleep easily. I was lying there in the hotel bed, and REALLY wanted to say a good prayer that night to thank God for finally giving up a positive-sounding visit. I'd asked Him the night before to PLEASE rebuild my broken spirit. I NEEDED some good news because I was just–dying inside. I don't even know how to describe it beyond that without keeping everyone reading for hours. So I got what I asked for! I closed my eyes, and I said, "God I'm really tired and don't feel good, so if you only hear one thing before I fall asleep, hear this–Thank you. Thank you so m. . . . z z z z z z z z! Yes, I passed out on the Creator of the universe. (Don't worry. I think He forgave me–I found a dime on the ground the next day). Lol

Friday, we got up and visited a Harley Davidson shop and ate at this adorable little outdoor Greek Café. This is unrelated to cancer, but I feel appalled enough to share; I ordered a Caesar salad and they SERIOUSLY did NOT have Caesar salad. In my shock I exclaimed "You don't have Caesar salad???? Wasn't Julius Caesar GREEK?! Dad thinks he was Roman. I'll ask Jeeves. ANYWAY, back to the story.

So we left the café and headed to the surgeon's appointment. He walked in, discussed the situation with us, asked me questions, looked at the scars from the last surgery, and then said, "Well, that's going to have to come out". If I were a screecher–my jaw would have hit the ground at that moment. And this man was looking at me as if he were delivering BAD news! I wanted to pick him up and dance around the room with him! Lol The surgeon left the room to "give us a few minutes to decide" (what decision IS there here?) and mom went to the restroom. The door shut—I looked at Dad—and he LITERALLY started jumping up and down! He pumped his fist in the air and rubbed his hands together like he was watching wrestling. Then he grabbed my hand and rubbed his hands together over it too, and my knuckles turned red. I think there was so much excitement in Dad at that moment, that there WAS no way to get it all out. Then he pulled me up and hugged me so tight I thought perhaps we could skip surgery and he would just SQUEEZE the tumor out. Didn't happen. Oh well. Mom returned and he hugged her too. The surgeon returned and we discussed possible dates for surgery, and then he shook my hand and left. We walked out of that hospital with 10,000 brick buildings lifted off of us. Dad was jovial. Like a court jester. I can only describe it as playful and light like a bird. I've NEVER seen him like that. Mom kept calm. She's not the "jumping up and down" type. I think it would hurt her back. She also likes to really process things before she reacts. She's good like that.

So I was thinking about this–and the joy I saw in my parents that day. Ya know–I colored a LOT of pictures for them when I was little. I picked at least 500 dandelions for my mother. I got good grades. I graduated. I got some stuff into art shows–I REALLY made my parents proud a lot throughout my life. And STILL–after all that I DID the one thing that made them happiest was the thought that they wouldn't have to lose me! I don't say this in a conceited way–but maybe it's like this for most parents. It's not about what we DO–it's just about having us, knowing us, watching us BE. Maybe that's what being a parent is all about–maybe it's about helping build that person, and then just being proud to know them because they're a part of you. That would make sense.

Reflection 10
Outcome of Surgery—September 20, 2009

Well, here I am at St. Mary's Hospital in Rochester, Minnesota. They got all the cancer out of me and had to take some of the middle lobe of my lung and a piece of my diaphragm. I had an epidural, so haven't been feeling much pain until today. I'm just sore and achy. They also had to break one of the bones of my ribcage, so that should be interesting to see how that heals up.

Other than that, that's about all we know so far. The surgery went AWESOME. I didn't have a repeat performance of that horrific experience from last time. The surgeon said it went perfectly, and he was done much quicker than expected. Everything has gone much better than we expected this time.

Now, let's just hope this cures me–or the oncologist gives me some chemo or something that will keep the cancer away. As of right now though, I am cancer free! I have thoughts to share, but there's an oxygen-measuring device stuck on my left index finger, so typing is very difficult. Thanks for your thoughts and prayers everyone! PS–It turns out the tumor was NOT attached to my heart.

Response Messages

BY MARY MILLER

Amber, we are so happy for you and have been keeping you in our prayers and will continue to pray for your cancer free recovery, you go girl!!!!! Uncle Royden and Aunt Mary

BY JULIE KAESTNER

Amber, I now believe in miracles! Amen! Love you. Aunt Julie

By Carmen Davis

YAAAAAAHHHHH! So HAPPY for ya gal!!!! Love you. Carmen

By Sandy Baker

Again. THANK YOU JESUS. Like your momma said, you are the Iron Bunny, AND you will WIN over this junk! Hugs, kisses and melon rubs from your ole #2

By Barb Freeman

Keep hanging' in there, Amber. We're with you. Love Aunt Barb and Uncle Austin

By Rick and Alexi Dawson

Yeah!! We must say that having found out the tumor was not attached to your heart was the most relieving thing evah!

By Peggy Miller

Fantastic Amber–I thank God and your Angels for some positive outcomes–"cancer free" are the two best words in the English vocabulary right now. Love you. Aunt Peggy

By Barb Fleege

Amber thanks so much for sharing your thoughts. I will copy this to Bob also as you know you are a huge mentor to him!!! Hang in there and hope yu have more times of peace than of anguish ASAP.

Reflection 11
The Next Step—October 12, 2009

Well, it was 89% against my will that we returned to Iowa City last Friday, but before you think this is going to be a bummer story, I'll skip to the end real quick and say that it really did turn around.

So back to the story. It was Friday, and we picked up our new friend from Iraq, Bushra. That was an interesting experience in itself which would turn into a TREMENDOUS sidebar story, so I'll refrain and just say she was really cool and felt compelled to hug me a lot. Lol what can I say? I was having a good hair day. Bushra had an appointment with an ear/nose/throat specialist in Iowa City, so she rode with us. Mom took her to her appointment and I checked in to Dr. Milhem's office. I had taken vitals, drawn blood, and was just about to go into a room to wait for the doctor by the time Mom got back, which wasn't long. They were moving really fast that day for once. Dr. Milhem came in almost immediately. I was slipping into a completely unnecessary panic attack, so my eyes had filled with tears which hadn't fallen out yet (thank God). So I was wiping my eyes, and he caught me. He kind of stared at me like he was about to ask why I was crying, but I guess I was convincing enough in making it look like I just had some thing in my eye (or both of them), and he seemed to forget about it . . .sort of.

He ended up deciding to do the same chemo I did last time. It killed 90% of the tumor that was in my lungs. You really can't argue with results like that. We're all still concerned about the neurological (brain) reaction I had with that chemo though. It's a drug called Ifosfomide, for those of you who have an interest or knowledge of cancer and such. The reaction is rare, but it happens to me, so it just goes to prove what a rarity I am. Sorry, I couldn't resist. Lol

Dr. Milhem is going to run this stuff called methylene blue, which sounds like toilet bowl cleaner to me, and I'm sure I miss-spelled it, which bothers me a lot, but it's this stuff that is supposed to bring me out of "crazy land" when I hallucinate. In the past, he has given it to me when I START going crazy. This time, he will start it at the same time he starts chemo, therefore trying to stop the reactions BEFORE they start, or at least shorten them. The first time, I was in LaLa Land for 3 days. Last time I was there for about 1 day. So with this third cannon being shot at the reactions, I'm sure it will be either 1 day again, or hopefully even shorter–or non-existent. I just hate freaking everyone out like that. They know I'm going to come out of it, because it's all completely reversible—but come on—who really LIKES the feeling of scaring the you-know-what out of your mother? I don't think I've enjoyed that since I was learning to drive?

He wants to do 4 more rounds of chemo. I admit this makes me feel fantastic. I honestly feel like I stand a chance now. My friend, Tom in the UK thought I was crazy for not IMMEDIATELY doing chemo when the cancer spread to my lungs. All this time I was doing clinical trials, I kept thinking of Tom, and thinking he was probably right. Tom, for those who don't know–had osteosarcoma that spread to his lungs. He has been cured now for 7 years. I take him very seriously when he states what treatment he received. Radiation is also up for consideration, although the radiation oncologist won't give me an answer for a while yet. Apparently, it's not really affective against sarcomas.

So if you're wondering why I was so reluctant to return to Iowa City, it's because I really wanted to switch my treatment to Mayo Clinic. However, Mayo Clinic couldn't get me in until October 20th. At that time, we would discuss our next plan of action. Then it would likely be another week before we actually started treatment. I really felt the need to start treatment sooner than that, and Iowa City was able and demanding to get me in sooner and is starting chemo the day after my appointment at Mayo. I was really just burned out on all the negativity. I realized a long time ago that staying positive is about ¼ of the battle when fighting an illness. I can't keep being reminded of my odds of survival. I am not in denial. I'm not being stupid. But I need to keep focused on the FIGHT–not the setbacks or the possibilities that I could fail. We told Dr. Milhem that when we went to Iowa City. Hopefully he respects that wish. I'm not emotionally made of steel, as those who have known me might have noticed. It's easy to make me feel really bad. If I HEAR it–it stays in my mind for hours. I really do ponder the strangest things for long periods of time. That's why I need him to stop reminding me of the negative possibilities. I could get hit by a drunk driver and paralyzed, but if somebody reminded me of that possibility every time I got in my car, I bet I would never drive again! It's not denial—it's just trying really hard not to DWELL on these negative possibilities—and I live down the street from 2 popular bars, so trust me—it's a possibility I'm sure.

Anyway, I'm relieved to know that I have treatment coming again. After a 90% tumor death rate, this could really be the THING that ultimately cures me of this monster.

For those who pray–keep doing it. It's working! I can actually see the haze of the light at the end of this tunnel–the light is possibilities that I haven't seen or been able to consider for almost 2 years now. Places to go, people to know, and a plethora of awesome foods to try and experiences, and knowing me–I'll probably grow my vocabulary too. I'm pretty impressed with my use of the word "plethora" just now. Lol

Response Messages

By Carmen Davis

You sound WONDERFUL! Stay positive!!! Love the pictures. I'm always praying.

By Barb Fleege

Keep up the great fight!!! We are praying for you Iron Bunny!

By Barbie Freeman

I love your description of not being in denial! Of course not! You just need to compartmentalize and put the necessary negative information in a different compartment from the one you live in most of the time. Denial sounds judgmental! What you're doing seems like positive coping. Way to advocate for yourself!

By Peggy Miller

Amber–I am so glad you were able to share your thoughts about "positive thinking" with the people in IC. Again, your thoughts reflect so much insight and patience with your treatment. Putting all of your writings together (in or-

der) would be a good start in creating an excellent "inspirational story". You have a gift Amber and so much to offer others. It was great to see you Sunday. Love. Aunt Peggy

Reflection 12
Thoughts of Children—October 15, 2009

I was writing to a single girlfriend on Facebook today, and the idea of kids came up. It makes me think . . . this is a big issue–one that I didn't know existed in the world of cancer until I got it myself. So I thought I'd copy my part of the conversation and share some of my thoughts on the issue with you all. The issue of my future with children is still something that rolls around in my mind a lot. Maybe it will never be put to sleep for me! Oh—and for squeamish people—no worries. There are no gross things in this blog. No "women's' issues" . . . just the one-time mention of eggs. Anyway, I cut out part of our conversation. And am adding some more of my thoughts to it as it applies to my personal issues here.

Kids. . . I can't have them. Chemo fried my eggs. They're sunny side down now. So instead of beating up on myself over it, I just imagine that everyone who DOES have kids is weird! Lol Sure! They're boring. They suck, haha just kidding. I've been thinking about it a lot lately. SERIOUS thinking. Because I think that your choice of wanting kids or not is important before you get into a relationship with someone. I've seen couples divorce because it turned out one partner didn't want kids. There's always adoption–but I read in a cancer book that a lot of agencies won't allow their children to be adopted out to people who've had cancer. I don't completely agree with this, but I also can't change it–at least not in my lifetime. They don't want the children to be re-orphaned basically when their adoptive parent dies of a cancer that returned. But children lose parents to natural deaths and car accidents all the time, so what are they really sparing the children? What if I'm cured RIGHT NOW at this very second and this cancer never comes back? What If????? It means an entire heart overfilled with love to give has just been wasted basically. But it almost seems as if the decision has been made FOR me, and as long as I've gone back and forth on this since I was 20, perhaps I should be grateful that I just don't have to think about it anymore.

On another note with that–I think I'm still too selfish for children. I like to come home from work and have SILENCE for like 2 hours. I like to sleep till like 11 on weekends. I'm random, inconsistent, spontaneous, and I can't imagine being any other way. Plus, I'm pathologically and unintentionally 15 minutes late everywhere, so how on earth will I ever get a kid to school on time?! So as maternal as I am, and as much love as I have to give, a big part of me thinks maybe I could spoil a husband and a cat or dog ROTTEN, and be perfectly happy. I sometimes feel something that appears to be my heart speaking very quiet, telling me it wants to get married and turn this world into our playground and run all over it, playing like children and taking goofy pictures in front of national monuments. It wants constant laughter and inside jokes and our yearly Christmas card showing us pretending to pick our noses in front of the Eiffel Tower. Kids don't fit into that scenario. But as the only child–I'm the end of the line. There's nobody to continue the Birmingham name. I'm my parents' only chance to become grandparent! They don't ACT like this is a huge deal to them . . . but maybe it is!

So it would seem that this whole issue is cleanly worked out in my mind and in my life. But my opposing thought on all this is . . . since I never decided if I wanted kids or not before I got cancer, do I really WANT kids, and this is just my mind's way of soothing me? Like . . . when you're told you're fired, and you say, "you can't fire me! I quit" . . . or you're told you can't have something and say, "whatever, I didn't want it anyway!" It's not true at all, but it's a form of self-soothing. You say it. You tell YOURSELF that. And then you BELIEVE it. And so the circle continues in my mind. Like I said–perhaps this issue will never truly be put to rest in my mind. I feel like I just want to peel back the top layer of my mind and peek into that next buried layer. I feel like I really NEED to see what's in there. I am baffled by the workings of my own mind. And now everyone probably thinks I'm crazy. I'm cool with that. Lol Crazy people shouldn't have kids right?!

By Devin Parker

It's a tough question. I'm 36 and I still think I'm too selfish to have kids. But I've also been told by good friends that you never "feel" ready to have kids. I agree with you in that your status with adoption agencies is unfair, despite understanding why they may have that policy. As you said, life is so uncertain, and it seems to me that it's better for a child to have the love of a parent than grow up a ward of the state or something. I guess one alternative for you would be to marry someone who already has kids.

By Rick and Alexi Dawson

Dearest Amber, We are all too selfish and crazy to have kids, but God still entrusted Rick and I with Squirrel Baby. May I suggest that you pray about it and trust God to guide you? Rick knew before he even asked me to marry him, I wanted to have lots of babies and adopt more of them and then homeschool them. Then, he still asked me (wasn't that nice?? knowing I would be with him when I choose to do this). I believe it is important to have children because we do value them, and we do value life. Non-Christians are having way more children than we are and we have to send our message out into the world to reach the people! As to the running over the world as though it was a playground…children ENABLE you to do that because they help you slow down to enjoy those things, otherwise we get too caught up in "me and life". Children keep you happy and young. Just think of those silly videos and photos I sent you of Freddy. Love us.

By Barb Fleege

Keep up the great fight!!! We are praying for you Iron Bunny! Love Barb and Bob

By JoLynn Deen

Well dude, first off…crazy people shouldn't have kids??? ummm…apparently someone forgot to remind God about me. But back to the topic at hand…though a VERY different situation, I also went back and forth on this subject for quite a while. And granted, God made that choice for me (and I thank him daily). I know that you will KNOW at some point. No one knows when or how but in your heart you will know. And when you know, I know, you won't let anyone stand in your way if that is what you want. How many more times can I put "know" in here? Whether or not you become a mom to a human child you were a born caretaker and you will have the luckiest husband in the world. Love you! Dude

Reflection 13
Birthday Weekend Chemo and Ifosfomide—October 29, 2009

Wednesday of last week was the start of chemo again. As I've mentioned before, Dr. Milhem and Dr. Okono (from Mayo Clinic) decided it would be best to continue with the Ifosfomide/Itoposide mix. We went into this somewhat expecting another neurological reaction to the Ifosfomide. Mom has asked me what I wanted her to do if I slipped away into LaLa Land, and we had a few plans in place. Let's face it–I was scared. To give you all some insight–the following is an Ifosfomide reaction seen from the eyes of me:

The first reaction lasted 3 days (they're only supposed to last 1-2 days). That was the time I fell and bruised my bad knee. I fell, and went completely silent for the next 3 days. I would simply grunt in response to "yes" or "no" questions. If I had to use the restroom, I'd simply start getting out of bed and expect Mom to follow suit and help me. I'm sure my eyes looked like there was no one in there. This is what was visible from the outside– this is what scared my mom.

From the inside, I was staring and staring at the TV. I was staring at soap operas and infomercials–both things I would sooner ram my head THROUGH the TV than waste a second watching it. But there I was … just staring. Lots of Billy Mays…"kinda thinkin" that pen that removes vehicle scratches might be on to something. Lol I wasn't thinking that THEN though. I was just gazing through the TV. It was moving. It was the only thing interacting on my very laze level of listening and understanding. It would talk and talk and I wouldn't have to say anything back. Oh the joy of that TV–with its flashing vibrant colors and mindless activities! I was transfixed. The other reason I was so transfixed was because when I stopped watching the TV, I'd lazily roll my eyes over toward Mom in her chair. . .and then slowly up to the ceiling. That's when I was laughing at the ceiling tiles. Some would just smile in a very dorky way–tongues hanging out, big exaggerated hands, eyes almost as large as their "heads" …Those who ever played the Super Nintendo Zelda and gone into a labyrinth, some of them have the floor tiles that flew up and tried to hit him. If you dodged them, they'd shatter against something, or you could hit them with your sword. Anyway, it reminds me a lot of that game. I had no sword… but these ceiling tiles weren't out to hit me–they were out to make fun of me! They were laughing and taunting and pointing. Some would look at me with these horrifically pitying looks and shake their heads and say, "Tisk, tisk my dear . . . not worth it!" There was too much action up there. Too much demand to awaken my emotions. Emotions at this point were a precious thing locked in a box.

Dr. Milhem would come in and tickle my feet, which I hated, but it slowly brought me back to Earth. He asked me where I'd gone, and I hadn't GONE anywhere…I stayed with my mom in LaLa Land. Perhaps I hallucinated wrong or something. Anyway, he proceeded to ask me where I was, who HE was, who was the president, who was my mom. Some of the questions I knew. I never knew the date. And I got Barak Obama's name mixed up with Osama Bin Laden. It has nothing to do with irony or my political opinions–their names just sound horribly alike in my head. Anyway, asking me who the president was kind of a bad question. I know who it is–but of course I gave the other name in my confused state. He let me slip back into LaLa Land and on Day 3 I was released, acting MOSTLY like myself again. On the drive home, I returned to LaLa Land one last time, and the clouds tried to reach down and get me to come with them. I just stared…they wanted me to join them! How fantastic…It was so beautiful, but I was just too tired to follow. It felt similar to falling in love…but I was just SO tired.

And that's an Ifosfomide reaction. Nowhere in there is Amber. Nowhere in all that confusion is the intelligent woman I spent my whole life becoming. There IS a very terrified little girl in there who felt bad—even in LaLa Land—for scaring her mother. Outside LaLa Land is a woman who never wants to go back. I admit–I always wondered in my teen years what the allure of hallucinatory street drugs was. I never tried it because the idea of playing with one's perception of reality is a very scary thing. But now I know. And I still don't see the allure.

So back to this last chemo. This time, they ran the methylene blue the entire time, and I had NO reaction. I kept expecting it. I was weepy in anticipation. My eyes became shifty and were starting to make strange patterns out of the lines of everything. No opinionated ceiling tiles though. The clouds were silent as they drifted by…The only noteworthy event of that chemo was on Saturday night when I was walking to the bathroom. I remember walking in, sitting down, peeing, getting up. . . EXTREME light headedness. Then chomping down in my mouth–that feeling that you've rammed into something hard. My rear hit something–I must've sat down very hard. The next think I know I'm on the ground, hysterical, screaming, "Oh God! Oh God! Oh God"! over and over. I think that's all I knew to scream. I was in Dad's lap (halfway). He was telling me to calm down. Take deep breaths. I don't remember him pulling the help cord out of the bathroom wall, although he did in his frantic need to get help. I don't remember the nurses coming; I only remember them BEING there. They moved me sideways into a chair immediately outside the bathroom. I was still screaming. I was afraid my leg would bend over the armrest and …I don't know… kill me maybe. They may have given me pain shots or done an examination at that time–I don't remember and I wouldn't have felt it anyway. The next thing I know I'm back in bed. I cried for a while longer. I believe I was in some sort of stunned shock for a while. At some point they took x-rays although I don't remember that either. The verdict; my bad knee was fractured. Bruising was spreading fast. At present–the whole thing is still a lovely deep purple.

Tentatively, surgery is at the end of next week. That should give me a week to recover, and then I'm planning a much needed escape to Louisiana to meet some new friends and help an old one. There is little to worry about here. I got lucky. I didn't return to LaLa Land, and my knee will be repaired. And I am blessed with a father who loves me enough to watch me scream even though it hurts him too, to look boldly at what could've been very gross, and feel bad for not being there when I fell. What more could he have done though? I was in the bathroom! It kind of applies to life; we can't always be there to catch our children when they fall unfortunately. But he was there in the aftermath, and that's exactly where I needed him. Thanks Dad. As the "quick status" says–I was released from the hospital on Sunday morning. The hospital had a little cake delivered to my room before I left, plus a nurse brought me in a piece of cake Saturday night. We went to Taki Steakhouse for my birthday dinner, but that's another tale for another time. Two tales in one day! I'd say that's plenty!

Amber and her dad, Terry.

Response Messages

By Brett Larson

So sorry to hear about your knee. Hope surgery goes well and I'm glad to hear you have a fun trip planned! You need all the R & R you can get after all you've been through. So glad your reaction to the chemo was better than last time. We'll keep sending prayers your way! Charlene and Brett

By Barb Newhart

Dang girl that was one strange experience! I'm glad you didn't have a repeat. Bummer about the knee too. Talk about adding insult to injury. Hope surgery goes well and you're up and at 'em in no time!

By Devin Parker

Wow–freaky-deaky. Yeah, I think that pretty much clears up any curiosity I may have had about hallucinogens. Doesn't sound like a lot of fun?

Amber's Response to Devin

Trust me, Zero fun. Except for hearing"Feelin' Groovy" by Simon and Garfunkel every time the reaction started again.

Reflection 14
The End of Chemo—December 3, 2009

A lot of you may have already heard the main news through the grapevine (or through ME); Dr. Milhem decided not to continue giving me chemo. I am really not sure how I feel about this. Hence the reasons it took me so long to post about it. I was really silently encouraging my body to keep racing towards that finish line–6 chemos. The first 2 were pre-surgery. Then I did 2 more…then he pulled the plug on me. No more chemo. Those last 2 are just not gonna happen.

As it turns out, my kidneys really took a hit with chemo. My liver was also declining. They were not rebounding on their own quickly enough between chemo treatments. This could still be the cure for me though. The 2 pre-surgery chemo's killed 90% of the lung tumor. So I got 2 more after that–AND a very good surgical outcome. So …maybe this is it???? I really have no idea. Not sure what's going to happen. For some reason I've been floating on air lately though unexplainable bliss. We'll take that as a good sign.

Response Messages

BY JULIE KAESTNER

You crack me up! Of course, we here in Atkins agree with the logic that the chemo got it all and the other two were just extras to help put it in in place! Love ya! Aunt Julie and gang

By Barb Newhart

Ditto what Julie said. And I agree with you on the bliss-definitely a good sign. In reality, none of us knows what's going to happen. And, if you can be blissful in this frickin cold weather, then it must be good!!

Reflection 15
The Latest—December 18, 2009

For those who are unaware, on Tuesday, I went back to the oncologist for a CT scan to conclude the chemo I just finished. It was a standard thing they do at the end of most chemo treatments. I panicked to the point where my chest hurt several times waiting for the results of that scan, yet to a certain extent–logic was telling me there was nothing to worry about. I was over-reacting and that is NO surprise to those who know me well. In my heart I knew we'd all be laughing at how much I panicked later.

Dr. Milhem walked into the room. Asked how I was doing. I told him the good news that the surgeon had decided I don't need knee repair surgery. He sat back with one leg crossed over the other–leaning back. He said, "Well I have bad news". My heart fell straight out of my chest, through the tiled floor, through the 3 floors below us…through to China and into the bowels of hell is probably where it landed. My mind shut off. The explanation continued. All I could hear was his low voice…and a very jovial and over-animated one in my head saying, "See! Always listen to ME. I am always always right." My eyes clouded up with tears, but it was a very delayed reaction. He'd been explaining for a few minutes by then. "There are 6 new lesions. They're on both lungs now. Surgery is no longer an option"…All I remember is not wanting to blink. Because if the tears fall–it meant I was really crying…a ridiculous technicality I started believing as a kid. Before the crying DID become official though, I made sure to look him in the eye and say, "thank you so much for trying". It sounds really cheesy I'm sure, but I happen to know this man has spent 2 years now trying every waking moment to cure me. He's just as upset over it as I am undoubtedly. I know he probably spent a lot of time leading up to this (in the years and months prior) worrying that if he couldn't cure me, I would blame him. And I don't. But somehow I'm just not surprised. The first and second time it came back, I remember it felt like a javelin being shoved through my heart when he told me. This time it felt like…NOTHING. Everything dies there will be no trying a different car, no trying different jobs until I find a career I like (well–I like what I've done, but was hoping to gain some new experience), no having children, and most importantly–no looking back on a long life well-lived and giggling with my friends when we're all spunky old ladies. All those dreams almost VISIBLY fell out of the sky and crashed on the floor in front of me. Cancer won…it seriously WON. In that moment, I wished I had never been born. At least then I would never know what I was missing out on.

He wants to start me on a drug for rheumatoid arthritis. I'd spend 5 days in the hospital every other week indefinitely. Until he either finds something better, the spots grow, OR my body craps out and some random organ starts showing strain. At least I'm alive……right!?

I was kind of a zombie Wednesday. Today, I am more myself again. I see all of my dreams as "most likely not possible" instead of "flat out not gonna happen". An improvement I guess. He made it clear he wasn't actually calling me incurable "yet", but sent me home to "enjoy Christmas" and let him do a little more searching around, and then we'd get back together and discuss it. But osteosarcoma has never been cured without cutting it out of a person before, and mine has decided it's going to be recurrent, so it'll likely just keep coming back.

My faith and hope jars were emptied Tuesday. I can only be my most honest and genuine self, and that is what is honest and genuine. And to be honest, it was almost a bit of a relief. For 2 years, I've forced myself to believe I'd be cured of this thing, and 5 times now, I've had my spirit absolutely shattered. I don't have to pick it back up off the ground and glue it back together now! No more roller-coaster! Faith is a heavy torch to carry for 2 years, and I will no longer look like a fool to people who see me vehemently arguing for and believing in something that is clearly NOT happening. Allow me to clarify–I still believe in God, but I feel betrayed and disappointed. And HE is aware of this. If you're going to have a relationship with someone, be prepared to tell them when they've thoroughly pissed you off and hurt you. For all who have asked how they can help, there are really only a few things that would make a HUE and positive difference for me. For Christmas, if you're family, please just don't bring it up at the Christmas gatherings. I know you care, and I respect that, and even appreciate it. However—from my point of view—this is the worst thing that has ever happened to me and it's the worst thing that has ever happened to my parents. It's ALMOST inescapable in our heads though. I mean it with ALL love and respect, that for now I just don't want to discuss it. Besides what is written here–I don't know anything anyway. I don't even know when I'm going back to the oncologist. This doesn't mean I never want to discuss it again–just give me Christmas.

Also, I feel fine. So anyone who sees me, don't hug me good-bye as if you're doing it for the last time. There will be other hugs. And maybe. Although I'm not even letting my heart get worked up again. There will be a cure soon.

Christians–I love you dearly, I'm ONE OF YOU, but alas. Please don't bother sending me a Bible verse. Those are the WORDS of God. Only GOD can fix this at this point, and He has chosen not to. When I say I am hurting and someone simply flings a Bible verse at me, I feel like I'm knocking on your door to get out of a blizzard, and you just slammed it in my face. Besides–it's the context that matters HUGELY in scripture. And often, I'm noticing it's taken out of context. The Bible says the world will end one day in Revelation–taken out of context, you could probably convince me that it will happen in 15 minutes. Make sense? Again–there is no way to say that without sounding rude. I don't mean it to be rude. But when I hurt so bad inside, I can do nothing but tell others how to hurt me LESS until I'm emotionally built up inside again.

Last–just give me a week or so to absorb all this mentally. I'll bounce back. I promise. This is just a very hard pill to swallow. It's big and jagged–and my throat is closed up choking on it at the moment. We can talk about it, and I'm open to questions—but like I said—just not when I'm attempting to enjoy Christmas. Oh–and currently, I do NOT wish I'd never been born. I do feel like my life was an anticlimactic waste though. I am SO sorry if I have offended anyone here. My blatant honesty can be a great strength–but can also be a devastating bulldozer. Know that I love and appreciate everyone who has been here for me. I'm simply stating needs here

Response Messages

By Ryan Birmingham

I hope that you know that I love you very much. It sounds so cliché saying it after everyone else that commented said the same thing, but I really really do. It really makes me sad that your faith is going down the path of disappointment and doubt. But it is understandable…I get it. I want you to know that you can count on me for WHATEVER you would possibly need and ANYTHING you would want to do. Not to brag, but I've always been pretty good at not bringing certain things up in front of you. I love you Amber Birmingham…You will always and forever be my older sister and without that I don't think I would be who I am today. You ignited my passion for imagination and creativity which has now thrown me down the writing path. That's pretty important. And you basically shaped the type of man I will marry…..oh Leonardo Vicario.

By Marsha Snethen

I think it is okay to let people know what you want and I think they don't mind. They can never know what you are going through else they have not gone through it themselves. I find that I don't know what to say to people that are hurting inside and I don't want to upset them anymore than they are. (I know this is soooo different) but when Jessica died people kept asking me how I was and I got sick of people asking me that. I guess I just thought people would know that I was feeling so many different things. I knew that people cared a lot, and they didn't know what else to say but (how are you doing) so keep telling people what you want and keep your heart happy and the other things will fall into place. We love you so much Amber. Love you, Marsha

Reflection 16
Just Something—December 30, 2009

I don't have much to update right now. Just wanted to say a few things. Christmas (with the exception of one late gathering), is over now. And I wanted to thank you all for respecting my request—for both my sake and my parents'—to not talk about the cancer thing over Christmas. Often times it's what a person SAYS or DOES that shows they care. But this time, it was in the things that WEREN'T said. I only had this conversation twice over the course of 4 Christmases, and THAT was very bearable. So again– thank you so much for that.

Second item–we scheduled my next appointment with Dr. Milhem. January 5th at 9:00 a.m. He went ahead and scheduled me to start the Methotrexate that day, but also sent me an email of 2 clinical trials available at Memorial Sloan Kettering, which is in Manhattan. I'd have to go there to receive those. He'll discuss those options with me on the 5th as well. So I'm scheduled to start the drug—BUT—I can go ahead and just cancel that if I decide to try one of the clinical trials. Obviously, it is far easier to cancel something than it is to try and squeeze yourself in once they are booked.

My spirits are in a strange place I cannot even begin to describe. My heart is in a cloud. A very warm and soft cloud. It's safe from all this. But my brain seems to have kicked into overdrive. It wants to avenge this! It wants to demand WHY? What caused this? It wants to know the precise second and the exact thing I was doing when this began. I told Mom the other day that I bet I get to Heaven and God tells me what it was, and the whole time, it was something I loved doing IMMENSELY, and something so ironic, that I will just collapse in tears when I hear how close I could've come to saving myself. But then Mom said there are no tears in Heaven. Except mine I guess. I imagine I will have to be sedated by Cupid's evil twin with his flaming bow and arrow before they will be able to drag me out of this world. I started praying again a few days ago, but made it clear to God that my faith is still almost non-existent. I admit–I raised an eyebrow at the email about the clinical trials. But that was about it. I haven't hung any faith on them working…haven't hung any faith on the Methotrexate working either. And the last part of the whole human (well, for the sake of keeping this short–I could REALLY write a novel on my views of THAT), my soul. My soul is better off left alone by most people right now. It feels like a newspaper some kid crumpled up and held a match to just to see if the tiny flame would ignite the giant ball. And when it didn't ignite…threw it in the street. A lot is actually being said in that seemingly odd or meaningless analogy. But I'll leave it up to the reader to ponder. So "how am I doing" is a very hard question to answer right now. It completely depends on how you mean it. Physically, I am doing ok. I am alive. I really have no answer beyond that. This may sound very strange–but I live almost completely outside of myself now. I can hardly bear to look at the train wreck that IS how I'm doing. My heart is fantastic. Let's just talk about what goes on in there for now.

I have a very strange insomnia. Like I am afraid to miss out on any of the end of my life. I am awake frantically cleaning until 1-3 a.m., and then I awake around 9:00 a.m. I am exhausted most of the day, but can't sit still. I clean like CRAZY–either that or I'm gone. It's as if cleaning this apartment until my hands bleed from bleach is REALLY going to stop this cancer from getting me. It sure FEELS that way. So I proceed! There's always SOMETHING to do. I usually take something to MAKE me go to sleep once it starts getting into the ridiculously late hours although my apartment is very clean!

Maybe it's NOT over for me. We'll see what these clinical trials are all about. I am completely exhausted though, so hopefully my insomnia has ended for today. At least I am feeling better than a week or two ago when I found all this out!

SO THE JOURNEY CONTINUES. TO WHERE? I HAVE NO IDEA!

Reflection 17
Expectations?—February 2010

I've been doing some thinking. I feel myself closing up sometimes. I think I had a revelation tonight in my complete exhausted mental haze. Since these thoughts are still so vague and intangible…bear with me as I attempt to stumble through them. And excuse the use of the word "expectations"… it's really due to a lack of a clearer way to put it right now.

When I was told I had cancer, everyone expected me to be devastated. And I was. Everyone is "expected" to act in a certain way at that point. For example, in a funeral setting, everyone wears dark colors, some people cry, you send flowers to the funeral home, and a sympathy card to the family, attend the funeral, feel sad, etc. Those are the standard actions to take. With cancer, of course there were the calls and visits and (oh dear lord) THE HOME-MADE CHICKEN AND NOODLES (I'm salivating, just a sec. lol). I'm not really sure what "standard procedure" is with cancer, but I THINK EVERYONE MANAGED TO BE SUPPORTIVE AND GET THROUGH ALL THAT. Each time the cancer came back, though, I think the "expectations" line got more and more blurry. I know a lot of people wondered "is it ok if we still call?" or "does she want to talk about it?" Because there was a gung-ho let's go kick cancer's **** parade in January of 2008, and each time the cancer returned, the parade got quieter and quieter. People no longer knew what to say. We'd skipped that chapter in the "How to Treat a Cancer Patient" book. And sadly, I have been little or no help. It took a few hours of complete silence in the solitude of my own apartment to see that.

Now that I've been told I'm inoperable…I don't even know what anybody expects of me. And I certainly don't know what to expect or ask of THEM. People ask me about cancer and I realize I instantly clam up. I am either very short with people, I stumble over words, or I say I don't know. And if I say I don't know, it's the truth. Stuttering or stumbling a lot is a nervous thing I do by accident. But why so clammy all of a sudden? Are these not the same supportive people who were there in 2008? I think what has changed is not everyone else–it's ME. I am 25 now. What is expected of a 25 year old woman? Well…it could be any number of things…most of the 25 year old women I know are married, a lot have a child by now. Or there's the opposite route of dancing drunkenly on a bar in a mini skirt (clearly

NOT married). They're career women. They have 1001 lives. Their "hourglass" has not started draining in their mind, and it totally shows. There's a relaxed clarity in the eyes of someone who has never stared death in the face–is not CURRENTLY staring death in the face. Death is more than a pesky little bother. Death is a ball and chain you drag around that clenches into your ankle with each step. Sometimes it wears so heavily on me that I just feel exhausted to my core–even if I haven't done much physically all day.

I guess what I'm trying to say here, is that I don't feel like I'm living up to the expectations of a 25 year old. When I'm addressed with cancer questions, I think I clam up because it's unnatural. You don't ask a 2 year old how death is coming along basically. That's for people in their 90's…people who've lived a long life and are ready to meet their maker. I'm nowhere close to ready to meet mine. I admire my girlfriends to death…I just don't feel like I'm living up to the same standard as they are most of the time.

On the flip-side of this expectation coin, I've noticed a lot has happened post-cancer that I never expected. I found love. REAL love. Not just butterflies. But someone who cares about me as much as I care about them. I always thought that once a person got cancer, their romantic life was over. It was all about "The Fight" from then on. But allow me to elaborate for just a moment here…and hopefully I won't nauseate anyone. When I can take ALL this intense energy that IS Amber Birmingham, and put it towards worrying about death and cancer, that is a horrible and torturous thing. Now that Luke is around, I have something positive to put some of that energy toward. It is a wonderful and healthy thing for me. I realize relationships are work, I really do. But it turns out they don't require the same kind OR the same amount of work I was putting into them before. Things sail along for us. I'm happy, and I NEVER expected to be romantically happy. I had almost settled myself to just being alone, because I DO have an incredibly fun time by myself…just better with somebody to share it! I also had my eye on the building every time I drove by. I thought the spiral staircases were awesome. I always wanted to live there…and lo and behold! I got to live in the building I always thought was awesome POST cancer. Hell! I never even thought I'd get to move back out of my parents' house again! People are coming together, mending old relationship so they can work together too. We've had lots of fundraisers for me and for general sarcoma research. I'm truly glad to be the one that started all that. I don't even know how many people are affected by this now that I'm thinking about it. Is it …touching them??? Or is it INFECTING them? I honestly have no idea.

My final thought tonight (for this topic anyway), is that nobody knows what to say around me. As of tonight, I realize we're all in the same boat. I have no idea either. I try to talk about it, and I'm morbid. I FEEL morbid. I have an incredibly cavalier attitude towards earth right now. And maybe it's just "screw it" mentality, or maybe its serenity. Either way, I understand a lot of other people don't live with that ball and chain every day. When I say something very casual about death, it IS shocking. I will try to keep that in mind. However, I really don't know what to say if not my honest thoughts about things. I'm curious to know what anybody else thinks about the expectations thing. It's ok to tell me I'm being over-analytical. Because I do that daily. Lol

Chemo starts Sunday (tentatively). Going to see Luke on February 14th. Chemo again (tentatively) on February 23rd. That's about all I have for update right now.

Response Messages

By Barb Fleege

Amber, I think it is wonderful that you can open up like this. It really helps to have you do this as it is difficult to talk face to face about it. I will look forward to seeing you and your mom next Tuesday with Bog.

By Rick and Alexi Dawson

I think Amber, when I think of talking to you, I think, I want to know how she is feeling, because that contributes a lot to her attitude, and then I want to know and talk about Amber. Not about what she is facing or dealing with because that isn't you. You are Auntie Amber–Auntie to Squirrel Baby and MGG (mysterious Gift from God) and you crack me up. If your time here is short I don't want to waste it inquiring about your cancer the whole time. That means I better be getting to know you better! I am so glad you have been feeling better. Because we love you and miss you terribly.

By Devin Parker

All I can say is it's about bloody time somebody finally opened their eyes and realized you were there. Bravo, Luke whoever-you-are. I'm glad to hear your spirits are up. To be honest, I was so busy trying to play it cool at Thanksgiving that I realized I didn't really say a whole lot to you while you were there. Sorry about that.

By Peggy Miller

Great to hear that news. I pray this is the time for a breakthrough for the clinical trials and a new treatment is discovered!! I heard you had a terrific time in the exciting parade. A fantastic experience. Love Aunt Peggy

Reflection 18
I Made a Change—March 2010

Monday, I returned from another week with Luke. I was on edge because of a lot of things–the biggest being my scan on Tuesday. It was a routine CT scan of my chest, but as many of you have probably noticed by reading my blogs or just watching my life–there is a definite pattern here. ALWAYS bad news. With that said, hopefully most of you can understand why I was regrettably a complete spaz to my family and my boyfriend in the two weeks leading up to said scan, and also why I took incredibly deep offense to somebody who felt compelled to tell me that "miracles" don't always look like we expect them to.

A quick rundown of what's BEEN going on leading up to this. I've been on a chemo called methotrexate. It involved me being hospitalized every OTHER week for 5 days. This left me with virtually NO free time. I'd get out of the hospital exhausted from being waked up at 4 AM every day, and spend my week off trying desperately to cram my missing week into it. For anyone who's ever tried to do that even once or twice–maybe you noticed it's close to impossible. I was also experiencing guilt for constantly leaving my cat with friends or driving him all the way to I-Town and letting my parents keep him. That's hard on him, and I wasn't able to care for him. When I WAS out of the hospital, I was never around. Sure–he's just a cat.

But I took on that responsibility 5 years ago when I adopted him, and there I was running all over and neglecting that responsibility.

After the first scan on methotrexate, we discovered that the spots in my lungs were still growing, much to my surprise and disappointment. My oncologist raised my dosage. Now on top of sitting for 5 agonizing days in the hospital every other week, I was beginning to feel like it was also a waste. I admit I have avoided posting on Facebook or anywhere else lately because I've been walking around getting increasingly angrier. I'm not myself lately–not even close. I find constant reminders all around me of everything I've lost to this ****. And it just keeps taking and taking. What more does it want? It seems like the only thing that will stop it is the epitome of my happiness itself. Because I've given everything else at one time or another. This isn't a self-pitying attitude. Not once have I felt SORRY for myself. I'm pissed! Outraged! How dare this thing barge in to MY life which was going perfectly fine, and just wreak havoc?! If anything, I want to fight it HARDER. But I didn't feel like the methotrexate was fighting it very hard. I guess that's what I was attempting to get back around to saying.

So Tuesday morning, Dad went with me to the hospital. I was scanned at 7:30 and got my results that afternoon. The spots are STILL growing. How can I even feel surprised anymore at this point? This is why I say I'm not myself anymore. I'm almost…apathetic…lethargic. Not completely sure how to describe how I am toward the continuing flow of bad news. Just lay it on me. But don't make me wait. The wait kills me. I was given the option to either continue with the methotrexate on a higher dose since it MAY have been slowing the growth (but not stopping it), OR, I could switch to another chemo. It's outpatient. I'd have more time to live life again. And maybe THIS chemo could be the one that actually stops the growth! Once my oncologist told me that we'd still be able to go back on the methotrexate if this doesn't work, I was sold on the idea. I get to lose the inch of hair I'd built up (and this is why I just cover my head all the time. I didn't want to get my hopes up about having hair again, but that's for another blog some day).

I don't honestly know how I feel. I took my first dose yesterday afternoon. I had an anxiety attack last night because I wasn't sure I'd made the right decision. Was I thinking with logic, or was I thinking with the dread of further boredom and loss of time? I think the ultimate goal here IS to stop the tumor growth as opposed to just slowing it down. So in that respect, I think I might have made a good choice. Sadly, I DID look at that hair and I AM in pain over losing it now. I'm sure I'll get over it. If it was really JUST hair, more women would shave their head out of choice. On the bright side, this will allow me to spend TWO weeks with Luke instead of just one at a time. I can also take friends to chemo with me or go by myself instead of sucking up all Moms' time off from work. Sorry–no loud kegger's ladies. I DO share a chemo suite usually. I need to somehow improve my outlook again…So that's my change. Thanks for listening and caring everyone.

Reflection 19
The Near Future—April 2010

Today I was sent to Methodist Hospital for Platelets. I tried to talk my oncologist out of it because I felt perfectly fine, but he wasn't comfortable with it. Basically, if they're 10 or below, it's critical. They were 7.1 and I was just happy they weren't 2 like last time! Lol In the long run, Mom and Dad were glad to go because I got a nosebleed last night that took 15-20 minutes to stop. It was the worst one I've ever had in my life too. Was on the laptop and suddenly my face was just covered in blood. Looked like I had been trying to teach Chuck Norris a lesson! I say a scab or something was in my nose–but they insist it is Armageddon and a sure sign my platelets were too low and I was going to get another one in my sleep and bleed to death via my face. Nice huh? Personally, I thought that'd make a great obituary. "Amber Birmingham passed away in her home Sunday night due to complications from trying to fight Chuck Norris. Mr. Norris could not be reached for comment due to ongoing hospitalization and permanent paralysis."

In other news, I'm supposed to have yet another scan in about 2 weeks. We don't have a date for it yet, but it's coming. Dr. Milhem wanted to lower my dosage of chemo since I handled it so badly last time, but I talked him into continuing to be as aggressive as possible. He was really bothered that my platelets had hit 2 last time. At that level, it is possible to have a stroke.

 I understand his concern, but I get so livid that this cancer keeps ruining everything. It keeps interrupting my life and the sanctity of my good nature. I'll be in a great mood for weeks and then BAM–I see or hear something that reminds me of the life growing inside me, and it's not a baby. It's a HORRIBLE life growing inside me. It's a parasite that wants to kill me, and it's winning. I want to hurt it badly. I want to do sick and twisted things to it and make it suffer for what it did to me. It brings out an anger that I wasn't aware I could reach! So "going easy" on it just isn't an option to me. I told Dr. Milhem that if something has to kill me young, it's just not going to be cancer. At this point, I'd almost rather die from low blood counts or whatever–anything just as long as this cancer doesn't get the privilege of taking me from this world. It's much like election time and you realize you don't really like any of the candidates–but one stands out that just sucks so bad that you'd do anything to make sure THEY don't win it. Let some other idiot win, but you're voting AGAINST them. Yeah. It's like that. Anything is welcome to try and take me–but cancer isn't winning this one. So I took another dose of the same amount this last time. I'm glad I did too, because I handled it better. I wasn't nearly as achy and weak. I never got so light-headed I couldn't walk around. My worst days only lasted 2 days instead of 3 this time…I was assertive which is something I'm working on, and it worked out well this time. As for the scan in 2 weeks–it'll show us if this chemo is even working. If it is, my oncologist is still considering lowering my dosage, but I'm going to keep arguing it I think.

I also lost my hair last week. The first time it was devastating. The second time I was under the impression it was a "trade-off" of sorts with God (I'll give you my hair if you cure me)…the third time…I'm numb. Yet somehow hurt so deeply over it. There IS no trade off. And I really don't know if I'll ever see my hair again–or if it even matters. It's certainly not JUST hair… it sickens me to remember all the money I spent on that gorgeous hair and how it just shriveled up and died right before my eyes. Chemo kills the hair and makes it look really straw-like before it falls out. It's hard not to be really resentful about that. I was raised to know that if you take really good care of your things, they stay nice…Boy has adulthood taught me that very little of what I learned as a kid is true. I've spent a lot of time just sorting things like that out in my mind and TRYING to maintain a good attitude. It's really hard when I haven't had a ponytail in 2 years. A wig can't be swept up into an elegant style for a really formal night out either…I just get so tired of giving and giving and giving of myself for this cancer, and it just keeps taking. When will the CANCER give up and die? What on Earth did I do to deserve this? I believe in Karma…what goes around comes around…so this came around to me…why? Seriously. Why?

Despite this blog, I'm actually in good spirits today. I've been doing some things for myself today. Things JUST for me. JUST to make me happy.

Time Reflection 20
Time Just Stopped For a Moment—May 2010

Not much to say today, but I HAVE been pressed for updates, so here it is:

Chemo is tomorrow. It's the drug that makes me ache really badly, although I find myself fortunate to be on something that doesn't make me sick. The steroid is enough to make me go out of my mind, and I'm supposed to start taking them again today. If you see a crazed woman in a green wig streaking frantically through an airport or something, please gently stop me and remind me that the steroid feeling will pass–and give me a pill to calm that obnoxious side effect. Knowing me, I WOULD end up streaking if I went crazy. Lol What can I say? I'm memorable.

For those who haven't heard–this OUTPATIENT chemo is actually WORKING! My tumors either stayed the same size or SHRUNK!!!!! There are 6. If I remember right, 3 of them went from 11mm down to 8mm. One of them went from 10mm down to 8mm, and the rest remained the same size. My friend Abbey had the same result when she took NOTHING for like 4 months now, and her tumors are STILL not growing. She said she cried when she found out they'd shrunk…I didn't. I didn't really react at ALL actually! Just as if I'd gotten bad news, we quickly skimmed over the topic and started talking about the *Ride it Out for Amber*, and joking around. Looking back, I'm a bit astonished at my lack of reaction. I've wanted this for SO LONG. Maybe I just don't trust good news anymore. I was instantly taken back in my mind to Mayo Clinic–not so very long ago. And in my mind I saw Dad just as clearly as if he were right in front of me again—wearing jeans and an orange T-Shirt, jumping up and down because Dr. Deschamps was willing to cut the cancer out of me—again. I saw the smile, the rubbing of his hands together…everything. A whole memory in just an instant. And then I was back in the present. And it was sobering I admit. Everyone knows by now how THAT good news ended. Come to think of it I don't think I reacted THEN either! Maybe I've gone numb or something. Think of it this way; how many hills can you withstand on a roller coaster before you get tired of the jolt to your stomach, and just want to get off? I'm an avid coaster fan…but I think if I rode one endlessly for a whole day, I'd be tired and nauseous. So I'm really hoping this chemo continues to work–maybe even makes me operable. And when/if it does, it will be a quiet victory–not the loud screaming party we all had the first time. Because I'm tired inside from it. I immediately called Dad, Luke, and Grandpa with the news. By that point, I WAS excited. I WANT to believe this is the path to curing me; I just don't want the disappointment again.

I was just going through some pictures, seeing if there were any to add to my Facebook, and I came across a small envelope very innocently labeled "2/13/08". In my heart, I had a feeling what was inside the envelope, because I remember very clearly what happened that night…but in my head I was thinking "no way! Could it BE?" I opened the envelope and into my hand fell a clump of silky soft reddish brown hair…MY hair! My ORIGINAL hair! And it still smells like shampoo, and the tip curled out on one of the pieces. I was stunned! I had no idea this hair was saved! A lump rose in my throat, but I didn't cry. Really…this feels like being reunited with someone you haven't seen in FOREVER. I can't believe there's still evidence of the original Amber! So often I feel as if she's buried under what people expect to be the "New Amber". But OLD Amber really wasn't so bad! Sure she was completely spineless, and never stood up for herself, but she was NICE! and GENUINE! And this hair was her style. A lot of people don't realize just how important your hair really is. Even if you choose to be bald. The way you style your hair whether male or female–is a direct display of your style. There is a REASON you keep it long, short, layered, dyed, pulled up, braided, spiked, etc. So yes–this IS an envelope of OLD Amber, and I'm grateful to see her again. I'd love to BE her again, but with a gimp leg, a port, and a variety of wigs, one must be a lot more tough and less…"taking BS", for lack of a better way to say it. Old Amber's biggest fault was that she was too soft. I DO like the new me…I just miss that hair…ALL that lovely hair.

In other news, I'm headed to a chiropractor for an assumed pinched nerve that's been bugging me for about a month now and I am keeping busy teaching myself to cook some new dishes. Baking is my forte, so I want to expand into cooking.

Personal Messages

By Mae Kaestner

So glad to hear the encouraging news. I pray it will continue in the good direction and that you will be given peace and patience for the day ahead.

By Peggy Miller

Good to hear from you Amber–I am still trying to understand what it must feel like to be in your reality! I agree–too much excitement makes disappointment even more difficult. Silently I am thrilled–openly I send my love.

By Carmen Davis

Wow—you have a right to be angry—it's just NOT FAIR! Everyone at the Legion is rootin' for YOU! We love ya gal, stay strong!

By Brett Larson

Hi, glad to hear there's another chemo that you can try although again we're also sad to hear that the other treatment wasn't working well. It's no wonder that it's impossibly hard to keep your spirits up through all of this. We keep you in our prayers daily.

By Bob Newhart

I don't know whether to hope I see the crazed Amber or not. Lol! I can't imagine your roller coaster and I absolutely hate them, literally and figuratively. The picture of Old Amber must be bittersweet–however, I must say that Rickie sure is a handsome guy! Hope to run into you soon.

Reflection 21
Chemo Cut Short (Possibly)—June 2010

I don't have long to write this time, but we just got out of an appointment with my oncologist. He is concerned about my blood counts, and has lowered the dosage of one of my drugs. He's also saying I will have another scan on June 15, 2010. At that time, we will determine if I will get my last 2 doses of this chemo, or if I'll switch to a pill that will "stabilize" everything as he puts it. I'd get 2 months to grow hair, play and have fun. Be non-chemoy….That would be amazing.

Trying to plan a trip right now, so if I didn't have to worry about chemo or any of the stuff back here for a week or two…that would be incredible. Sure my body appears to be "maxing out" on this chemo, which sucks. But right now I feel optimistic.

That's all for now. I'm about to start another round of chemo. I also have to go to John Stoddard Cancer Center tomorrow for another transfusion and a shot, so I'm a busy girl today and tomorrow. In the meantime, I've got a painting haunting my brain, so it's gonna have to come out very soon! Just have to buy the paints, which equals an entire DAY in the crafts store! Lol.

More soon

Response Messages

By Marsha Snethen

Thinking about you each day. Keep up your spirits. We love you Amber.

By Mae Kaestner

May God's peace that passes all human understanding be with you now and in the days to come. Stay strong in your faith. Love Mae

Amber getting ready to participate in an annual Ride it Out for Amber.

Reflection 22
Chuck Norris and a Scan—June 2010

Sorry it has taken me so long to get on here and tell everybody how meeting Chuck Norris went. I've been busy beyond belief!

We were one of the first people to show up at the rally. It was held in this giant auditorium and we got wrist bands and things started moving forward from that point on. We got in a line that lead to a little room that was completely empty…except for a photographer, Chuck Norris, his wife, the candidate, and the candidate's wife! Mom, Dad and I walked in and shook hands with everybody and posed for a picture. Then they rushed us back out so the next people could get a picture taken.

Next, we got in a REALLY long line and the candidate came out, followed by Chuck Norris, and the rally began. I'm no Republican, but even I thought it was exciting hearing everyone get all psyched up to vote for that guy! Like you could feel the excitement in the AIR! I couldn't stand long because I was extremely weak from chemo that day, so I had to keep sitting. I sat down next to a girl about my age that appeared to have Downs

Syndrome. She had an ENORMOUS ring on every finger and held her hands up to the light and just kept wiggling her fingers in it and smiling… for some reason I was a bit mesmerized by her. Her actions seemed symbolic to what I'm going through in my life; in the midst of all the action going on that SHE didn't understand…she simply went somewhere else mentally! I guess there is something to be learned from everyone in life.

Finally the rally ended, and the line went down and I joined my parents. They'd brought my T-Shirt for *Ride it Out for Amber* and were going to have him autograph it and get some pictures on our camera for Facebook and everything. When it was our turn, he gladly signed the shirt, put his arm around me, we posed…and THE CAMERA DIED! No problem. We had MY camera too. Chuck put his arm back around me…we smiled… AND THE CAMERA RAN OUT OF BATTERIES! No problem! We got one more camera. Chuck put his arm around me again, we smiled…waited…AND THAT CAMERA WAS OUT OF BATTERIES TOO! My God. What a time for the cameras to die. Lol so that's the reason there are no Facebook pics of this. Mom freaked a little, but Dad reminded her that we got that professional photo with Chuck in the little room, and they are supposed to mail it to us.

For lack of mental energy to think of a better Segway…I'm going to talk about something else now. Lol Tuesday is my next scan. I'm not really sure what to think. I'm starting to become very nervous. My mind is wandering around to all the "what ifs". It SEEMS relatively safe. But then it has before too, and I was blindsided. Being blindsided again is just something I can't handle with everything else right now. I've been looking at my life up till now. Where have I messed up? Who do I need to apologize to in life? I mean who REALLY deserves an apology from me? I tend to apologize to people who couldn't care less that I'm sorry. And I've been thinking about who I should be more appreciative of. Life just seems to have passed me by and I feel like I took it all for granted. I've spent it pursuing dead ends, and resenting anyone who tried to stop me. I've been a doormat to an extreme point. I have hurt my friends who don't understand why I don't answer my phone, and to be honest, my inability to answer it is a problem too. There is a laundry list of things I'm realizing I've done wrong in my short life. I'll leave it at what I've just said.

I also find myself wondering what the entire point of my existence is. God I've pondered that hard lately. When I was 15, I decided to start dating, because I was SURE my entire purpose was to love and BE loved. I wanted to get married and have a family and be the BEST most supportive wife ever. But that has worked out HORRIBLY although many important lessons were learned along the way, and that idea has been weakened a bit over the years. I honestly do not think anyone male OR female—family, friend or boyfriend—has felt more love in their life as a result of knowing me. I leave my boyfriends angry and bitter and they never remember the love I brought them…and I find myself crying a little out of frustration right now because it seems like everyone I've tried to show love to–I messed it up and it turned to anger. If I left this world tonight, it saddens me to think of all the anger I'd leave in peoples' hearts. I also thought I was sent here to create art, but I've neglected my passion horribly. And I'm an environmentalist– what have I really done for the environment besides recycle? If my purpose in life was any of those 3 things, then I have failed miserably up to this point. Before anyone assumes I'm walking around depressed all the time, there are also the thoughts of my future. Do I HAVE one? Is it too late to fix everything I've done wrong in life? What will I do if I am told I have to go back on the methotrexate and I have to go back to staying in the hospital for 5 days at a time?????? I'm really worried about that. If this chemo worked, can I finish my regimen? Could I really be cured some day? Could I finally leave Iowa some day?

Sorry for the long post. My mind is in a very deep place lately, and I think I just rambled straight from my heart, which is weird since this is not a private forum Lol. I just want to be ok with that scan on Tuesday, and I'm scared.

I am still learning to cook. Mastered pasta salad this week. Thinking some sort of soup will be my next project. I don't know though. It's kind of hot out for soup. We'll see! Preparations for *Ride It Out for Amber* are still ongoing. I hope we have good weather, because this thing will be HUGE if it's nice out!

Response Messages

By Rick and Alexi Dawson

Chuck should have roundhouse kicked your camera, and then it would have worked.

By Barb Newhart

What a rush to meet Chuck Norris! Wow! Keeping all digits crossed and prayers said for your scan. I can really cross them all too–cross my heart! Lol

By Barb Fleege

Let's focus on GOOD WEATHER for June 26th! Thanks for sharing! Bob and Barb

Update from Mom
June, 2010

Good morning family and friends! I have not been writing much on here lately because Amber has been doing an awesome job keeping everyone updated. I just wanted to remind everyone about Amber's ride/drive this Saturday, June 26th. This is our big annual fund raiser we've been doing for the last three years. It raises funds for Amber and also brings awareness to Sarcoma. We have met some awesome people on this journey and we want to honor them as well. This year we are so blessed to have other young people who are also fighting this cancer along with us on the ride. Not sure how many can come but I do know there will be a few. Dr. Mo and some of his staff will be riding with us again this year. It will start in Indianola at the garage and end in Polk City at our post again this year. Registration starts at 9:00 a.m. and we leave at 10:00 a.m. We should be back at the post by 4:00–4:30 for those of you that just want to come to the auction and fun at the end. If anyone would like a flier with more info please let me know and we'll get it right to you. Also, please pass the word on to your friends and family that might not get this care page, we would love to have them. We will be riding rain or shine so join us in praying for a rain free day. Hope to see you all on Saturday!

Check out the picture of us with Chuck Norris. A lot of people have been asking me to post it. Sorry it took so long. This website has been down lately. I'll post about the *Third Annual Ride It Out for Amber* and post pictures and other updates a little later. At the moment, I just have a hellacious case of writers' block. I've made myself sit here for almost an hour trying to produce a readable update for everyone, but my brain is just spitting out cartoon characters and stuff I need to get done…and then there's the open window behind me.

OH! And the trip to Omaha. There are a lot of updates. Sorry, I know a lot of people would like to know, but I'll have to post a little later. I get the impression that my brain just doesn't produce writing before midnight. Much Love.

Update from Mom
July 2010

The HuHot restaurant in Ankeny saw Amber's write up in the Juice magazine and called and told her they will give 10% of their proceeds to the Sarcoma Foundation in her name on July 12th. We are so excited about this. Anyone that would like to have a nice evening out for supper and support a great foundation please come out and join us. Terry, Amber and I will be there the whole time. It is the Ankeny location only.

Quick update here guys. Amber goes for a blood check today but all seems to be going real well for her on this new drug. She is really able to enjoy her summer because this doesn't seem to be making her sick at all. Thank God!

Response Messages

By Barb Newhart

Amber I'm so glad to hear this doesn't seem to be making you sick this time. Hope everyone enjoyed HuHot–I've never tried it, but those who have raved about it!

By Colleen Baker

Sounds great to me–we love that place!

By Becky Carter

Been looking for a reason to go there again!!! We will be there!

Reflection 23
Florida—August 2010

Well, I finally made it to Florida to meet my new friends, Rusty and Ralin. They are hilarious! I arrived Friday, and have "maybe" stopped laughing for a total of an hour since then. Their little girl is 3 and was my instant buddy. We've been reading <u>The Three Little Pigs</u> and I introduced her to Led Zeppelin's "Stairway to Heaven" as every 3 year old should be.

This summer is everything I could have asked for. I finally got to go back to life without the physical part of cancer. And the mental part has mostly been on a backburner in my mind all summer. I have spent a TON of time with my best friend, Raeanne. I went to Omaha Zoo with Rae and our mutual friend, Greg. I got to enjoy the *Ride it Out for Amber* ride and gorge on as much junk food as I pleased without chemo-induced mouth sores. Jo and Mark were there, and I hadn't seen Jo forever. It was kind of like old times. I was practically attached to her hip because we get together and don't shut up. Lol. I also got to meet Codileigh, another gal with Sarcoma Cancer. She lost her foot to it, but like me, she just proudly walks around like a drunken pirate, and God help you for making fun of it. Lol Codi was pretty cool. I only wish I'd been able to talk more with her. It was really crowded though and I had to mingle.

Of course there was the Juice article, which ended up having a ripple effect. It led to the HuHot thing and tons more people knowing about Sarcoma Cancer. It ended up being FAR bigger than I ever could have expected.

For those who know about my breakup in May, I am way sorry I was such a downer for a few months there. The good news is I am ok now! I took some ME time and figured out exactly how I felt about the guy, and how I feel about myself, and also how I feel about dating again. In the end, I hadn't made a decision. The decision was made for me when I couldn't stop eyeing a certain somebody. I was flirting and laughing again and hadn't even realized that those old GOOD emotions had snuck back up on me again! I had been FIGHTING that! Yet there I was, smitten again. At the end of July, my new interest flew to Iowa to visit. A few days into his visit, I decided to stop fighting what I felt, and told him I would be exclusive with him.

The thing you should all know about dating, and love, and breakup, is that I don't break up like a normal person. When I experience a breakup, I feel INTENSELY rushed to hurry up and feel better and be over it. There are feelings of guilt for wasting time feeling sad, I was blessed with this summer of freedom, yet I was crying myself to sleep every single night. I knew I should be grateful and not sad, but there is no separation there. There is no compartment in my head labeled "these emotions are strictly about the breakup" and "these emotions are strictly about cancer". They all ooze together. So feeling sad about the breakup made me feel GUILTY and like I was being ungrateful about the time I had away from chemo. I really hope this makes at least a little sense. It's very important in understanding what I experience with cancer. This oozing of emotions also seems to hinder my ability to deal with the breakup in a healthy way. On the flip side—when falling in love, it feels like I only have about 5 minutes to piece together an entire life with somebody—from meeting to marriage. That is a tremendous pressure on me AND the relationship, and I fight it. In the last relationship, I admit that was hard. Not because my ex pressured me, but because HE was just as excited about our life together as I was! I think we fed off of each other's excitement. He may have other theories, but I digress. This time, I am encouraging my new boyfriend to take things at a healthy pace. I like him a lot. I want this to be a healthy thing for both of us…we can wait for each other.

Since this is getting long, I'll wrap it up for now. I'm in Jacksonville, I'm with good people, I'm having the time of my life, and I've already made a few new friends. This place is stunning in its beauty and the only shadow over it all, is my scan on Tuesday. I cannot get it off my mind. I don't know what else to say. As enjoyable as this time away from chemo has been. I can't help but want more.

Reflection 24
What Just Happened?—August 2010

A few weeks ago I had my scan as scheduled. Unfortunately, it showed that the tumors are growing again. As if that weren't bad enough, there is also a new spot on my lung. I took this news in stride, as if he'd just informed me that carrots are orange, but in my stomach, an epic battle was starting. I felt it tense up, and then nausea. Mom continued asking questions as if nothing was wrong. The events occurring around me didn't seem to match the new reality I'd just been presented with. I didn't see Mom react with shock, or even flinch. When Dr. Milhem finally left the room, Mom went to call Dad. I looked around the tiny room I was in, it literally felt like those walls were closing in on me–ready to melt down on me in moments. I noticed my heart speed up. Its beat was SO intense inside me. My hands were sweating, and I wiped them on my jeans. Then I started to cry. I suddenly felt a hopelessness that almost can't be described. The tears didn't come gradually like they usually do with me. Instead they just poured out like a broken dam. I can't believe it still–but I let myself sit there and sob like a child. The emotions were childlike, I felt like it wasn't fair that the pill didn't work. I NEEDED more time off chemo. I NEEDED time to re-connect with ME and just be away from that horrible place. The feeling of being trapped welled up inside me too. Honestly, those few moments of sobbing were just awful. I was admitting to myself that I AM a prisoner and cancer is my jailer. Despite the acts, the NOT discussing it, the discomfort with the questions—it's still THERE—laughing at me as I continue to try and escape it.

Then two things happened simultaneously, Mom returned and George text messaged me. I stopped crying. Mom asked me if she'd left me for too long, I said no. A nurse came in. She commented that she'd walked in on this far too many times (a patient sobbing). I gave her the excuse that I was just tired…I really don't know why I felt the need to make an excuse for crying at that moment. I'm just so uncomfortable with being caught doing it. The whole time we were talking to the nurse, I was thinking about what I'd tell George when I responded to his text message. He wanted to know the results of the scan. He was at work. I didn't want him to have to deal with awful news so soon in our relationship. It's only been about a month! Finally I decided that the only way he'll ever adjust to being in my life—my REAL life that involves the cancer—was to just lay it on him. I texted him exactly what happened. He seemed really concerned, but I suddenly found myself more concerned with cushioning the blow of the news for him. In a strange way, I was able to go back to being myself (taking care of other people) simply because I didn't want HIM to freak out. Something that is so important to understand–giving the bad news is SO hard for me. I WANT everyone to be able to cheer and be excited about my health. I get a high off of that! The looks of disappointment, of disbelief, or anger even–I don't know how to deal with any of that except to smooth over it and blow the bad news off like it's nothing. Also, as it turns out, Mom just doesn't react anymore because she doesn't want to get ME upset, or give in to hopelessness.

So I went back on chemo that day. The steroids are kicking my @$$, but otherwise I'm fine. Got a flight booked to Louisiana for George's birthday now that we have a chemo schedule established. I'm really excited to meet his family and do a little more traveling. That is my focus right now–the positives in life. Sure I'm surrounded by a Shit storm right now, but coming from a girl who can't run anymore due to the knee replacement–sometimes it's nice to walk slowly through the rain and savor.

Response Message

By Marsha Snethen

Amber, cry when you feel the need. I think it helps with the stress that you are feeling and gives you a new look on things. We are always praying for you. We all love you.

Reflection 25
Not Completely Unexpected—October 2010

Last week was quite a week for me, and this week has been too. Tuesday, I had another CT scan scheduled. It showed that all the tumors in my lungs had grown. I admit, I'm just so emotionally tired and had just begun to feel the slightest glimmering of what could be called hope. The tears just fell out of me. It wasn't a "that sucks" cry though. It was a "please just let me sleep and wake up when this is over" cry. Dr. Mo told me to go ahead and cry, and probably expected me to cry a lot more, but I'm tired of crying too. After a few sniffles, I had my game face back on. He wanted to do another hard chemo on me, but first I needed an echocardiogram and a bone scan. The echo was gross. "The Girls" got all covered with ultrasound goo. The good news is that my heart is very strong and healthy. The bone scan (which he expected to show the cancer had spread back to my spine), showed NOTHING. This meant I was strong enough to take the next chemo. I was told to come back Friday to begin treatment.

Wednesday, George flew in to Kansas City. We found an O'Charley's for lunch and danced in the car all the way back to Iowa. I felt like I wanted to prepare him for Friday, but how do you prepare somebody for something like that? He was going to have to see some unpleasant things, and hear things from my doctor that might not sound very pleasant. My positivity is a CHOICE–and I was afraid he wouldn't be immediately able to make that same choice.

Friday came, and George, my dad and I headed to Iowa City. My doctor explained a little bit more about what we are going to be doing, and then I was able to start chemo. Dad and I fell asleep. George read a book . . . He seemed to handle everything ok. I'm proud of him. The days following have been crazy for my health. I've dealt with steroid issues, vomiting the first night and low blood counts which are making me extremely light headed. I share this only because I am so unbelievably shocked . . . he's taking care of me! The most shocking thing in this entire blog–I finally know what it is to be taken care of by someone NOT my family. And he's taken care of me despite the fact that I'm about to lose my hair again, and I haven't been able to take him to all the sight-seeing stuff we wanted to do, and I threw up in front of him 3 times, and he likely knows what all my pills do now, and I walk with a limp, and have asked him to run to the store for me so I could stay in my pajamas and cook. I've struggled with trying to shield him from it and having no choice but to BE cancery. I'm blessed. That's all I can say. I know I've been given a special gift here. That's about it. Tonight's special is chicken parmesan baked ziti with garlic bread.

Response Messages

By Barb Newhart

Girl that is an awesome man! How's that song go? "Hold on loosely, but don't let go…" I don't remember the rest, but this makes me think of that line. You're a true soldier. Un-cancery thoughts and prayers going your way!

By Barbie Freeman

Amber, I'm so sorry to hear about this crappy news! As I read, I was struck by how you are able to articulate not only your feelings, but also to attend to the feelings of your village of supporters. You continue to demonstrate a great depth of compassion for those around you. Cancer hasn't taken that from you. I also noted how you were able to attend to your needs as well as those of the people who care about you. By giving them directions about what you need…"just be normal"…you offer guidance to them. That's a gift from you to your village. I'll be thinking about you and yours this week.

By Mary Miller

So sorry to hear the outcome but want you to know that our thoughts and prayers are with you all and we are praying that Dr. Mo will find what he is looking for to help. Aunt Mary and Uncle Royden

By Mae Kaestner

I send my prayers and love. Your friend must be an angel sent from heaven. He is truly a gift. Take care and savor each moment.

By Marilyn Parker

That's awesome. I was really hoping he'd step up to the plate and I'm glad to hear he came through. Frankly, I figured he'd realize how lucky he was to have you, but it's nice to see my suspicions borne out. I'm also really glad to hear that the bone scan came back clean! That's great news. Take care!

By Peggy Miller

Amber, I will never decrease my hope–you continue to teach us all so much about life and the value of time and each other. I so enjoyed our time together and I am planning on making another big batch of potato soup. I so admire your spirit Amber. Love you, Aunt Peggy

Reflection 26
Just Putting it Out There.....November 2010

I wasn't really sure how to say this, and unfortunately I'm just going to have to dump it on everybody.

What was supposed to be a routine trip to the hospital yesterday for chemo turned into a day of bad news. My bad leg is swollen, so my doctor decided to do a biopsy on it. At the beginning of the day, everyone thought it was fluid. By the end of the day, all the doctors (about 10) who had looked at it were saying they thought it was more tumors. I was admitted to the hospital and received the biopsy and CT scan of my chest. The doctor on duty by the time my CT scan results were back told us that all the lung spots had grown, plus the cancer had spread to my liver, and the spot on my liver was pressing against the output valve of my heart–causing me to ALWAYS feel tired and have a little chest pain.

I spent yesterday feeling like a zombie–a total failure. I've been so strong all my life. I wasn't a sickly kid, my colds were always gone within a day or two, and when I was diagnosed with cancer, I was told that my body heals well and that would help me in the long run. It hasn't. Nothing has. The cancer is beating me. Despite fighting as hard as I can, nothing is working. I didn't even have the emotional energy to feel angry, and I still don't. If cancer takes my heart, it takes my ability to do anything for myself. And if that happens–I have truly given everything for this fight. My independence. I can't imagine life without it. Ultimately, without my independence, I am no longer myself. Am I making sense here? Cancer has invaded one of the most important parts of me!

Once we were given this news, the doctor decided I didn't need to spend the weekend in the hospital and let me go. I'm hanging out with my parents for a few days and was told to take it easy due to the heart thing. We are supposed to go back Tuesday to talk to my oncologist and get the results of the biopsy. He'll let us know what the next course of action is at that time too.

I lost my hope yesterday. I lost most of my faith too. I felt like God was making fun of me yesterday, and that hurt. Like any functional relationship–mine with God is a bit strained after all this. I honestly feel betrayed…it's not like I prayed for money or a car or life to be easier. I simply prayed that life would CONTINUE. For those of you in your 30's treasure that. I would give almost anything to live to 30. Hopefully I do. What I still have is my sense of humor. What I need from friends and family is to keep yours as well. And even though I've lost my hope–don't lose yours. Mine will eventually come back and you all help so much by just believing in me still. Know that I haven't quit fighting, and have no intentions of it. Most importantly, just be normal with me. Your jokes and such have pulled me through many rough patches over the past few years. And for those of you highly concerned with my spiritual well-being who felt likely crying at the beginning of this paragraph–God and I always make-up.

It's just a big "we'll see" right now. I'm dealing with some pretty intense thoughts and feelings. But now you know. And the good news is I got to leave the hospital, of course. Back to business as usual. Will tell you more as I know it.

Response Messages

By Barb Newhart

I can't speak for anyone else, but I still have a tough time wrapping my head around this one. However, God does seem to always work a miracle with Dr. Mo. So my prayers are going that way currently, and for you, your parents, the rest of your family and friends to have the strength, love and support that you need when you need it. I'd say let Chuck Norris go on that da*n cancer!

By Brett Larson

Sorry to hear about the latest test results. We haven't given up hope and we keep praying for you! It seems that there isn't any other way we could possibly help you but to keep praying–so we do! It's no surprise to me that your faith waivers because you've been through more than someone should ever have to go through and yet somehow you keep up that fighting spirit! Take care.

By Carmen Davis

Try as hard as you can to hold on to your hope and faith! I'm praying for you all the time, and keeping hope and faith. This might sound strange, but try to be grateful for all the healthy parts of your body and give thanks to them. It is the healthy that needs to overcome! I love ya gal.

A Final Post by Mom
December 8, 2010

As Jesus before her said . . . . . it is done.

Response Messages

By Carmen Davis

Amber, you are deeply missed by all on earth; heaven is blessed now with your presence.

By Callie Freeman

Jesus, calling out with a loud voice, said, "Father, into your hands I commit my spirit!" And having said this he breathed his last. Amber's spirit is in His hands, a great comfort as much as we will miss her.

By Devin Parker

I'm so sorry. Knowing that Amber's in His presence now is an indescribable comfort, though her company among us will be profoundly missed until we meet again.

By Monty and Lori Freeman

We have been continually impressed with Amber's courage and her way of meeting her disease head-on. She showed so much maturity and tenacity...I'm not sure I could do the same. She and her family are a wonder to me. Her poems were inspiring and saddening. Lots of Love, Lori and all

And finally, by Julie Kaestner

Well, as you can see if you've read Amber's writing that she was the writer in the family, not me. But, I do have many thoughts and memories that I would love to share if I can stop crying and get them down on this paper.

December 8, 2010, 5:40 a.m. never leaves my thoughts, and I still can't delete the message on my Hotmail account from my sister stating that Amber was gone. But, I'm smart enough to know that they don't have any significance anymore, because they won't bring Amber back to us. I don't have a need to visit her grave, because I believe that she isn't there anyway, but I KNOW that she is living with Jesus in Heaven, and THAT gives me the only peace that I can get.

I wasn't real hip on the idea of Amber using Facebook, to tell her thoughts and feelings. I didn't like hearing about her progress or little things that she shared on her page second hand. But to Amber, that wasn't second hand, it was straight from her heart and she wanted everyone to know it. As you know by now, that was Amber's way of talking. She never was a very talkative person, or even very responsive. You'd think, until you read her writings, she wasn't "saying" anything; because she was too busy "thinking" and "feeling". As far as my feelings getting hurt by hearing bad news on Facebook, wasn't her not feeling close to me…it was her feeling close to EVERYONE. Some of it might have just been the proud, out-dated aunt in me too. Smile.

I can't begin to recall of the lessons that I've learned from our family's journey with cancer, but one really sticks out daily. God has a plan for us. When we get frustrated that things are not going your way…God has a plan. When you are not happy with how you look or feel…God has a plan. When you feel that God has slapped you in the face and stomped on you…God has a plan. As Amber told us in her writings. <u>*"God and I always make up*</u>*". And that gives me the peace that I need to know that Amber isn't gone forever. Aunt Julie*

A Poem by Amber

The following poem was written by Amber not long before her passing. She was well aware of how close she was to a new life. The poem was read during Amber's memorial service and it has remained in my mind and heart ever since. Amber wrote:

A little spin on an old favorite…Excuse any slaughtering of spelling, grammar, or punctuation–this is what sometimes spews forth at 2 A.M. Lol

> T'was the night before chemo
> And all through the house
> Not a creature was stirring–
> Not even a mouse!
>
> The clothes were laid out by the bedsides with care–
> Knowing the cancer bitch soon would be there.
>
> With the world long passed out and my 2AM worries,
> I sprang from my bed to see what was the hurry!
>
> Oh it's just 2AM
> Why the hell a'int I sleeping?
> You think I won't kick cancer's ass while it's creeping?
>
> I quick called Chuck Norris.
> He'd know what to do!
> Then Spidey and Batman–
> We'd need his car too!
>
> We sped off in the dawn to find drugs that would
> WORK Surely there's a cure for this shit that won't hurt!

Amber Nicole Birmingham

We tried England, and Sydney, and Fifi, and France
But the drugs they had there gave me no better chance!

Finally we realized the only real way–
"On Spiderman, Chuck Norris, and Batman!" I say!

And that's when Chuck Norris came flying through air.
He drop kicked my ribcage–
The cancer was there.

And Spiderman zapped me with 6 tiny webs.
"One for each spot on your lungs," he had said.

Back to the batmobile.
Time to head home.
Chemo is early
Then it's "me vs. cancer------alone'

See you in a few hours, you heinous beast.
I've had some help!

Amber

Acknowledgements and Updates

1. Terry and Joelyn Birmingham: Continue to honor their daughter, Amber with their support of the annual *Ride it Out for Amber* events. This past year was the 7th annual fundraiser and proceeds still support sarcoma research. Family and friends support Terry and Joelyn in their activities and often speak of the inspiration Amber provided in her few short years. Information concerning activities to support sarcoma research or support for families in a similar journey may be obtained using the following Facebook sites and email:
www.facebook.com/RideItOutForAmber
www.facebook.com/SarcomaIowa
TBirmy@aol.com

2. Dr. Mohammed Milhem (Mo) still participates in annual fundraising for sarcoma research and remains a valued member of the University of Iowa Hospitals.

3. Amber's special cat, Ricardo, still lives with Terry and Joelyn and is adored as a special "connection".

4. A special thanks to Stella Smith and Ray Courter (Jr.) for careful editing.

5. Lee Jackson provided my inspiration for the theme and organization of Amber's writings.

6. Federman, D. (1990). **Modern Jeweler's Consumer Guide to Colored Gemstones**. (6th ed), Chicago: Vance Publishing Corporation.

7. A very special thank-you for the patience shown by Amber's family and friends waiting for the completion of her book. This was a heartfelt project for the author and at times difficult to continue.

About the Author

Peggy Miller is the great-aunt of Amber Birmingham. She was amazed with Amber's gift of insight and communication and often encouraged Amber to share her writings. Peggy is faculty emeriti with 37 years of teaching and service to Northwest Missouri State University in Maryville, Missouri. Since her retirement she continues to provide education and support to families who have lost custody of their children. Families are the most important unit of our society regardless of their functions, ethnicity, spiritual base or structure.

CPSIA information can be obtained at www.ICGtesting.com
Printed in the USA
LVOW07s1106040515

437128LV00002B/2/P